The Seafood Shack

Food & Tales from the
Scottish Highlands

INTERLINK BOOKS
An imprint of Interlink Publishing Group, Inc.
Northampton, Massachusetts

First published in 2021 by

INTERLINK BOOKS
An imprint of Interlink Publishing Group, Inc.
46 Crosby Street
Northampton, Massachusetts 01060
www.interlinkbooks.com

Published in the United Kingdom by
Kitchen Press, Scotland

Photography by Clair Irwin
except: Archive photography on pages 18–23
© Ullapool Museum Trust
Lobster fishing photography © Mike Guest
Additional author photography by Storm Curtis
Design by Andrew Forteath

Library of Congress Cataloging-in-Publication
Data available
ISBN 978-1-62371-910-4

Printed and bound in India

10 9 8 7 6 5 4 3 2 1

To download our complete 48-page, full-color
catalog, please visit www.interlinkbooks.com, or
send us an e-mail at: sales@interlinkbooks.com.

Contents

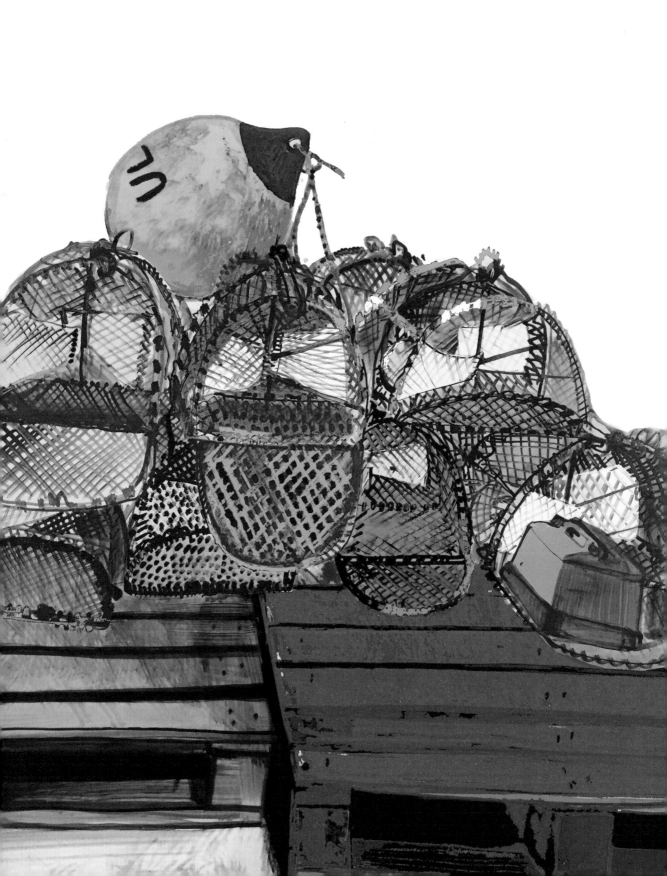

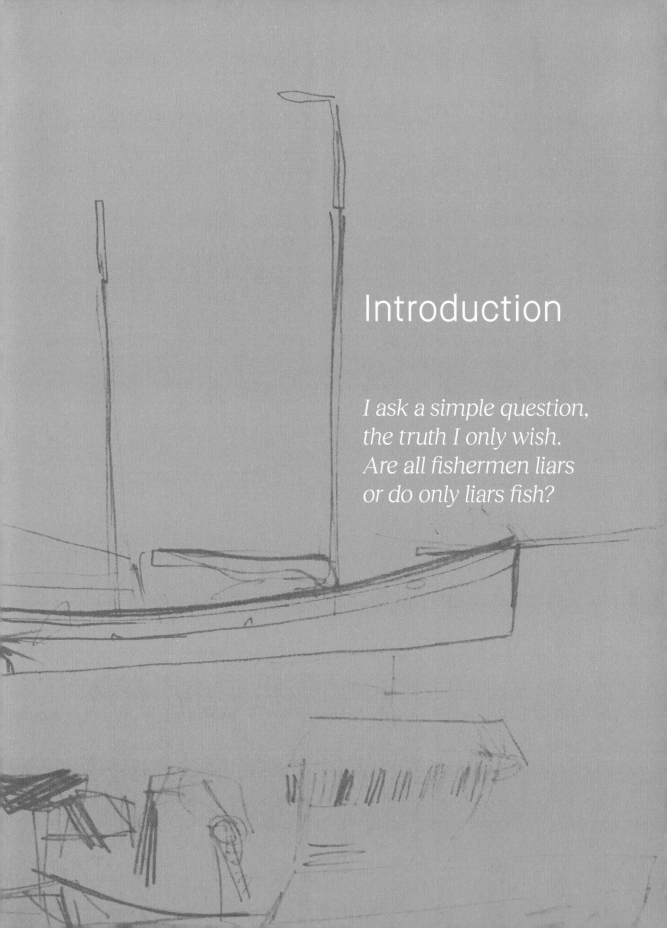

Introduction

I ask a simple question,
the truth I only wish.
Are all fishermen liars
or do only liars fish?

On May 3, 2016 we opened up The Seafood Shack in Ullapool. It was a very exciting day for us, our emotions veering from panic when somebody would come to order, laughter when things went wrong, and joy when we successfully closed up for the first day. In total we probably had 20 customers at most, but for us it was a great start to our new venture. We have kept The Seafood Shack a small business but we've now got around eight staff and are open seven months of the year, serving up to 300 customers a day. Really it's pretty amazing our wee Shack can cope sometimes, let alone us!

To this day we still have disagreements or "different memories" on how or when we decided to open The Seafood Shack but we both agree exactly on why. We both live in Ullapool, a small fishing village on the north-west coast of Scotland, where there are currently around seven local creel boats, four local trawling boats, and over a dozen visiting boats landing each week. Many tons of seafood are caught in our Scottish seas and then transported straight out of Ullapool. We wanted to play a part—albeit small—in keeping some of our seafood local.

We knew we had the produce supply sorted. We also knew that we didn't want the stress of large overheads that we'd have if we opened a restaurant, not to mention the pressure of surviving the winter months in Ullapool with little trade. It would be a huge financial strain for us to start up a restaurant, so we decided that a small catering "shack" was the way forward. The first thing to think about was the funding. There weren't any suitable grants we could apply for but with help from our family, our personal savings and the amazing support we got from the local community for our successful crowdfunding campaign, we managed to raise enough money to get the Shack started.

Next step was finding a location which we thought would be easy. As it turns out, what with all the rules and regulations about catering vans, not that easy! After lots of paperwork, planning applications, and things generally going wrong we finally found a perfect spot in the center of Ullapool—our own little courtyard which we still rent from Ullapool Harbour. While this was all going on and we didn't actually have a spot set in stone, we crossed our fingers and pushed on regardless. We ordered up our trailer which came from down south in Durham. Our friend Charlie is a great graphic designer and came up with our logo, so once our trailer arrived up in Ullapool we got it wrapped with a "shacky look" and plastered our new logo over it. The home improvement store B&Q was the next big stop, and Fenella's husband Mark and his friend Richard decked out the inside of the Shack. The summer soon crept up on us and on May 3, 2016 we opened up the hatches.

That first year, trading restrictions meant we weren't allowed to provide any seating, so we spent a lot of time trawling Pinterest and dreaming about what we'd have when we were allowed. When we opened up for our second season, we had installed our rustic tables and benches, and while some thanks is due to Pinterest for the inspiration, most goes out to our friends Dan and Tim, both highly skilled boat builders. We'd managed to find six huge old wooden spools that had previously been used for copper wiring from a company in Muir of Ord; they didn't want any money for them, we just had to somehow get them all back to Ullapool. So one day we both jumped in Josh's old van and whizzed down to Muir of Ord to do a few trips ferrying them all back up the road. We dumped them off with Dan and Tim who then transformed them into the tables and chairs that look so amazing in our wee courtyard today. It was genius.

Since then we have never looked back. Although the business is physically the same size, it has grown in so many ways. We are so glad that we didn't start a restaurant—what we really love is being behind the hatches, cooking away and chatting to our customers as they devour a haddock wrap or peel open some fresh buttery langoustines. We get a great sense of connection with our customers and the chat back and forth plays a huge part in our day-to-day life at work. We always have a laugh in the Shack and it's really important to us to keep it that way—a small business, without the stress of huge staff management, big business rates, pressure to make money in the quiet winter months and all the rest of it; we want to keep it fun! And if we can make a happy living from it then we're winning.

COLLECT HERE

Sweet cured herring served with salad, potato salad + bread £7.50

Pan-fried mackerel fillets in garlic butter, with wild rice + salad £8.50

OPEN 12 PM - 8 PM

A day in the life of the Shack is simple. We both arrive at work, Fenella at 9am and Kirsty (who has time management issues) soon after and we make a plan of what to cook that day. That plan is normally based on whatever Josh's fishing boat, *Bon Ami*, has dropped off earlier that morning. There's always some discussion with Josh at home either the night before or at five o'clock in the morning consisting of "please can we have four boxes of langoustines today" or "yes we'll take 24 lobsters tomorrow," but it's always changing and you're never quite sure what will be waiting for you at the Shack in the morning. Gary, our scallop diver, will randomly pop his head in any day and say, "I've got some scallops for you," and within an hour they'll be on the menu. Stephen, our fishmonger, is the one who's organized; twice a week we make a big white fish order with him and we always get the same reply. Every. Single. Time. "K"! Life really is that simple. Each week in the summer, Joe drops off a hundred fresh oysters and within a few days they'll be gone. We jump in the car once or twice a week to go to our local smokehouse to collect some smoked trout. We sell hundreds of delicious sides of their smoked trout each season. The trout is smoked in aged whisky barrels and cured in honey and it's honestly the most delicious smoked fish you will get. Ian, Graham, Val, and the team work flat out each year and we're all so grateful to them. These amazing people are a massive part of The Seafood Shack's success: at the end of the day we're not amazing chefs, we're just two girls who love to cook and having such fantastic and fresh produce is what makes the Shack work. And it's not just the seafood suppliers; we have many more amazing food suppliers and services that keep us running throughout the season. We would be lost without them. At the Shack we always try when possible to make sure everything we use is sustainably sourced, from the fish to the salad and, of course, our packaging. It was really important to us to get the packaging right as everything we do is takeaway so we get through a lot of containers, and the last thing we wanted to do was use horrible boxes made from plastic or polystyrene. We found a great company called Vegware who still supply us with all our packaging, cutlery, and napkins, all made out of plant-based, compostable material.

We feel so grateful that since opening the Shack we have been nominated for some fantastic awards. The highlight has to be being nominated for the Best Streetfood/Takeaway at the 2017 BBC Food and Farming Awards. When we found out we had made it to the top three takeaway venues in Britain we were just ecstatic! Romy Gill and Paula McIntyre came up to Ullapool to judge our food and as it was winter and the Shack was closed we had to do it in Kirsty's house. We had a great laugh with them and cooked them our best-selling dishes—it was a really lovely day and we didn't think things could get much better. So, months later, when we flew down to Bristol for the awards ceremony, we were completely blown away to hear our names announced as the winners. We were a new, small business from the Highlands of Scotland, so it took a while to sink in. Thank you so much to everyone who nominated us; you helped put us on the map.

We have also had some pretty amazing guests at the Shack. Our first celebrity guest appearance—which for us was very exciting—was Albert Roux. At the time he owned Chez Roux at the Inver Lodge Hotel just north of Ullapool so we had thought, to help us get some publicity, we would just write to him and see if he would stop by at the Shack. In all honesty we didn't actually think he would. But within a week we got an email back saying, yes, of course, Albert Roux would pop by on his way up north. The excitement was high and when he arrived for some reason we were both acting like two school girls. His one tip of the day was to NEVER rinse pasta after you've cooked it as it removes the starch and therefore lots of the flavor, and it stops that nice sticky texture you get in pasta dishes. But the main thing we remember was how amazing he smelled—pretty impressive for a man in his 80s. Honestly, the Shack smelled glorious for hours after he left.

The next exciting occasion at the Shack came in 2017 when Mary Berry visited us. We got a phone call from the BBC saying that they wanted to do some filming in Ullapool. Mary didn't initially want to come to the Shack at all; they were looking for a lovely west coast fishing village where she could cook up a feast on the beach using fresh seafood that had been caught earlier that day by a local fisherman, so it was Josh they were actually after. But after we signed Josh up (without actually asking him), we plucked up the courage to mention that we had a small business called The Seafood Shack and would they be interested in filming there at all? We didn't get a promising reply. But the BBC team came up a few months before filming and had a look at the Shack and seemed more interested, and at the end of the summer Mary herself finally came up to do a day of filming and did a scene with us. By complete luck it actually ended up on the show—Josh's fishing didn't even feature in the end. So if anyone who had some say in us being part of the show ever reads this, then thank you! We got amazing publicity from that and we will be forever grateful. Everyone asks us what Mary Berry was really like, and we've got to say she was in her mid-80s when she came to Ullapool and she worked non-stop filming from seven in the morning until seven at night. She never complained, she was constantly shooing her makeup artist away, and at one point we turned around to see her face completely black with midges, and she didn't even flinch. That is impressive.

We are incredibly proud of our wee Shack. There's no better feeling than walking into the courtyard and hearing everyone chatting away and enjoying the food. Every day we get to chat to both locals and people from all around the world traveling the Highlands and we only hope we have created some lovely memories for them.

Fenella

Alongside my three brothers, I grew up in a small but busy Highland village called Achmore. No internet or shops, but around 20 kids all about my own age. From the crack of dawn we would be running riot, not seeing our parents until we were hungry, and even then it was never your own parents who fed you—it was the closest house. When the World Cup was on we would have the grass cut and our homemade goals up with one of my dad's old fishing nets for the net. When Wimbledon was on we would have the net across the road, clearing it when a car came (that's how quiet Achmore was). We all knew it was home time when the streetlights went out.

My mom is originally from New Zealand and has run her own successful seafood restaurant in Kyle of Lochalsh for the last 30 years. My dad was a fisherman born and bred in Achmore, so fishing and seafood were always a big part of my childhood. From a young age my dad and I would be out on the boat catching queenies and crab, and I'd spend some of my summer holidays scraping barnacles off the bottom of his boat. Evenings would often be spent at the restaurant, waiting for mom to finish cooking, and I think being in that atmosphere with the smells, the noises, and the people enjoying the food gave me the drive to set up my own business. I met my husband, Mark, in 2007—he's a commercial diver and part-time fisherman—and we've now got two boys, Liam and Arthur. Life is always busy but I wouldn't have it any other way!

Kirsty

I was born and raised with my two sisters on a farm just outside Ullapool. We were completely off grid with our own water source and the house was run by a hydro generator. We grew up playing in hay bales, fishing in the river, and generally just running wild. We would always have to help with jobs on the farm and each Saturday was the dreaded changeover when we had to clean two vacation cottages and the big guest house. Our house was always full of people: we had workaways from New Zealand and Australia who would look after us while my parents ran the farm, so there was always lots going on. Dad was a keen deer stalker and would spend hours on the hill, and we grew up with venison as our staple diet; I think we've already eaten our lifetime's recommendation of red meat from Mom's meals. Seafood wasn't a big thing for us, apart from eating tiddly little brown trout from the loch below our house or, for a treat, a foul-hooked salmon from the river. It was such a busy house, and my mom had so much to do on the farm that she soon got tired of cooking for everyone, so from a young age my sisters and I were all put to work playing around in the kitchen. I've not stopped since.

When I was 19 I met my partner, Josh, who was and still is a mad keen fisherman and that's when I started learning lots more about seafood. Through my late teens and early 20s my jobs were always based around cooking—from working in a restaurant in Ullapool to cooking in a ski chalet in France. My main job though was as a lodge cook when I would be hired for a week to cook meals for parties of 14 all over Scotland. My love and passion for Scottish seafood really thrived through these summer seasons—I used to serve up huge platters of fresh langoustines, caught by Josh hours earlier, along with big bowls of buttery baby potatoes, a green salad, and some homemade mayonnaise. So simple and just the way people wanted them.

Point Street, Ull...

Ullapool's Fishing History

Looking out at Ullapool Harbour today, you'll see many different boats coming in and out to land: traditional and modern day boats that fish for lobsters, langoustines, and crabs; boats that go out and hand-dive for scallops; trawling boats that come in with tons of fresh white fish and shellfish; creel boats that go out for months at a time and line-caught white fish boats from Spain. But it wasn't always like this. Years ago, it was all about the "silver darlings," herring.

Opposite
Bob Jack, Andrew MacElman and John Mackenzie on Ullapool Pier, 1956

Above
Herring Girls Gutting, Point Street, (now West Shore Street) c. 1900

Ullapool was founded in 1788 by the British Fisheries Society with the intention of creating a new fishing port for herring. The society bought Ullapool Farm on the banks of Loch Broom from a Lord Macleod and began to attract settlers. These settlers were mostly fishermen, but there were also merchants, laborers, and tradesmen and each were allocated a small area of land with a house, vegetable plot, and a share in the common grazing.

By 1790 there were about 40 people employed locally in the fishing trade, and throughout herring season Ullapool was transformed into a busy community bustling with local fishermen going out to net for herring. The fishing grew and grew, until boats from all around Scotland and Ireland were coming to the west coast to take advantage of the thriving new trade.

Of course it was unsustainable, and by the early 1800s the herring stocks had drastically declined and the locals were forced to find alternative livelihoods. The fishermen began fishing from Caithness over to Stornoway, and local boats moved from Loch Broom out to the Minch. Although the British Fisheries Society founded Ullapool as a herring port, as the fishing declined it tried to establish new industries such as spinning, weaving, and agriculture. People were encouraged to become self-sufficient and land was made available to rent for growing crops or rearing animals. Despite these efforts, Ullapool struggled to withstand the loss of the herring industry.

Packing the herring
c.1900

There was widespread crop failure, locals began to move to Caithness, and the town sank into poverty. In 1847, when it became clear that the herring were not returning, the Fisheries Society sold Ullapool to James Matheson, a successful businessman who had also recently bought the Isle of Lewis, for £5000 (about $630,000 in today's money).

The community clung on. Herring pickled in brine was still a vital part of the local winter diet along with milk, oatmeal, and potatoes, so each summer fishermen would nervously wait for the arrival of the migrating herring shoals. It was always uncertain when they would arrive and often they would pass by too far out to be reached by the small local boats, to devastating effect. Although the inshore fishing was proving harder and harder, further out to sea herring were being caught commercially by Dutch boats who landed them in Ullapool and other west coast ports for processing, and this began to provide a new income for the locals. The fish would be split, gutted, and salted (white herring), or salted and smoked (red herring), and then packed in barrels to be shipped all over the world.

In the late 1800s trawling boats were introduced to Scotland and the fishing industry shifted to the east coast with Aberdeen as the main trawling port. Fishermen in Ullapool started looking towards lobster fishing, which was better suited to small boats that could only fish inshore, and was the first fishery squarely aimed at a wealthy market. By the early 1900s, 15% of Scottish creels were in the Loch Broom district —a much higher percentage than had ever been the case with herring netting or fishing lines.

But it wasn't all over for the herring trade. During the Second World War, mines made the North Sea grounds too hazardous to fish and, left to recover from years of overfishing, stocks of the "silver darlings" boomed. Post-war, Ullapool once more began to flourish, with so many east coast boats coming to fish the grounds that the pier needed to be extended. The return of the herring also brought the famous Klondykers to town. The original Klondykers were Scandinavian and Dutch cargo ships that came to buy herring landed by Scottish boats. They provided enormous employment for Ullapool locals since many people were needed to box and ice the fish before it was taken away to Norway, Africa, and the Canaries. The Klondykers would then return with fruits and delights from the markets abroad.

Ultimately this kind of intense fishing is always unsustainable, and by 1977 the stocks had again become so depleted that a total ban was placed on herring fishing. But this time around, the local industry was not so much in threat. Two years previously, long before the end of the Cold War, factory ships from the Eastern Bloc had begun to come to Ullapool to process mackerel—a staple food in East Germany and the USSR because of its nutritional value. On occasion up to 70 of these factory ships would be moored in Loch Broom, an amazing sight which was often met with disbelief by visitors. To add to it, they were sometimes joined by Nigerian, Irish, French, and even Japanese Klondykers: everyone wanted to be part of the mackerel jackpot.

These boats were literally processing factories and they often stayed for up to six months of the year, increasing Ullapool's population by thousands. The crew would come ashore in small boats to buy up all the goods they couldn't get at home, and in the early days you would see them on the streets selling towels, shirts, fur hats, or handmade model ships for local currency. Even today some locals boast beautifully crafted ships in their windowsills. The collapse of the Soviet Union in the late 80s saw the beginning of the end of this strange and wonderful chapter in Ullapool's history, and the factory ships soon left. Many locals still miss the sight of the Klondykers in the bay, especially at night with their lights reflecting off the water, or at New Year when they would blast their sirens and send rockets into the sky.

Ullapool today is still a busy working port and arguably we have a much more diverse and sustainable way of fishing now. But in general the town no longer relies on the fishing industry: our main income now comes from tourism and the many opportunities that come with it. Locals can now retire earlier and run their own B&Bs from home, restaurants flourish through the summer months, gin distilleries are being created, the sea and the mountains are used for leisure and sport rather than fishing and farming, campsites are bustling, and cruise ships are the latest boats to land at our harbor. But although Ullapool has adapted and changed over time, the fishing industry remains at its heart and we locals are more and more conscious that we need to do everything we can to protect its legacy.

"We were very, very busy over the years with the Klondykers. It was in 1977 the first ones came— three came from Bulgaria. Some ships had up to 300, 400 crew on board. In latter years they were from Russia, Poland, East Germany, Bulgaria, Romania; there's some from Egypt and Nigeria over the years.

They came and anchored in the loch here and out by the Summer Isles. They didn't fish—it was the Scottish and Irish catch fleets that caught some herring but mostly mackerel and sold it to the Russians, or the Germans or Poles, whatever, for processing. Some of them were just filleting fish but others were salting, canning. They were factory ships, and then when they filled up transport ships would come from their country and would take the fish away to different destinations.

Klondykers at Ullapool Pier
c.1980

"Over the years it brought a vast amount to Ullapool, so many folk benefitted from it. Everyone got on very well. We got on famously with the Germans and the Russians and the rest of them—the Bulgarians, Romanians. Most folk—the restaurants, the pubs—made them most welcome because they were doing roaring business. And every other day they chartered buses and they'd go off to Inverness and do massive shoppings down there. They'd go to Argos and some of the other shops—Inverness did very well. They didn't directly employ people from Ullapool but there were always small boats and sea taxis running back and forth. There were a few who didn't like it, who complained about the noise and the smell, but it was not bad.

The beginning of the end was 1989 when the Berlin Wall came down and there was the unification of Germany. That was the finish of the East German ships because the East Germans started to become westernized and they didn't eat herring and mackerel as their basic diet—they were gunning for more Western foods.

Then the Scottish catching boats were getting bigger and bigger and the mackerel seemed to be getting further back. Before, they seemed to be thick around the Summer Isles but boats were having to go as far out as the Faroes to get the fish. Norway and Denmark started taking all of their fish back to their own factories, and also the Russian fleet was getting older and some of them weren't fit for their work any more. They were very much missed. Ullapool was like a ghost town in a way. At the height of the fishing there was between 7000 and 8000 Eastern Bloc people in Loch Broom. I remember seeing, between the factory ships and transport ships, 96 boats sitting out on the loch. It was amazing.

I still fish—we go out for mackerel. We don't get the haddock or cod any more. Back in the 70s the trawlers fished fairly close and they took all the fish. It's slowly coming back but it will take a while maybe."

John Macleod
Grocery Shop Owner

Buying Seafood

- Get to know your local fishmonger or fishermen. Start up a good relationship with your local fishmonger, just get online and see who's the closest to you; you might have to travel a bit to buy from them but if you do it once a week you can bulk buy for the rest of the week. If you're lucky enough to find a local fisherman then go have a chat with them and ask them if you can buy straight from them. You could set up a weekly or even monthly buy, or consider signing up to a fish box scheme (these are great, and you get a variety of fish delivered to your door).

- Avoid large supermarkets when possible. We understand it's convenient, but if you can it really helps your local fishermen and fishmongers if you make the effort to buy from them.

- If you can only get seafood from the supermarket, only buy fish that's been caught sustainably and locally—always check the label.

- Thinking of having fish for dinner? First thing to do is phone up your local fisherman or fishmonger and find out what's available! Don't plan anything until you know what you can get your hands on.

- Be prepared to pay slightly more for it. Local seafood might be more expensive but it's so worth it, and the fishing industry is under threat and they need our support. Think of it like buying organic, which people are prepared to pay more for because of its quality and sustainable, pesticide-free production methods. Local seafood is no different. Also, it's often the cheapest to you straight from the fishermen so if you can do this then that's great!!

- Buy more shellfish. Shellfish isn't that sought after and we really don't know why. It's totally delicious and full of tons of protein. We use a lot of shellfish— crustaceans (lobster, crab, langoustines, etc) and molluscs (scallops, mussels, and oysters)—in the Shack; it's just something we both love to cook, and living in Ullapool it's what's most accessible. There are so many small shellfish boats with local guys working on them it makes sense for us to use and support the produce that's available. Many of our friends and family don't cook with shellfish since it can be a bit daunting, so we hope this book helps show it's really not.

- Come prepared: take a suitable container with you. This means fishermen don't have the stress of trying to find something to put the produce in or stops the use of plastics from throwaway bags at the fishmongers.

- Know what you're buying. It's so important to know the different fishing methods since there may be some you don't agree with; for example scallops can be dredged or hand-dived, white fish can be line caught or trawled, shellfish can be creel caught or trawled, and the list goes on. There's never any harm in asking what method was used; after all we should all be aware of where our fish has come from.

- Avoid buying berried lobsters. It is illegal to sell them in many regions, and while it's not illegal in Scotland it is very much frowned upon. It's easy to spot a lobster with eggs: if she is female, she will have a much wider tail when turned upside down than a male lobster, with small flaps to secure and protect her eggs. If she's berried, you'll see thousands of teeny bright orange eggs tucked under the flaps. A lobster carrying eggs should always be returned to the water to ensure stocks are kept high.

- Stay informed, learn about your local seafood, and keep up to date with what's going on with the fishing industry.

- Mix up your fishy meals. Sometimes we seem to get stuck on the same fish: salmon, langoustines, tuna, haddock, and cod. Change things around—hake can be a great alternative to cod, or why not try trout instead of salmon, or splash out on some fresh lobsters or crab?

- And when you get it home, eat it all. So much gets wasted. You could treat yourself to a course and learn to fillet, then use the rest of your fish carcass for stock. Take time picking all the meat out of a crab, and turn your lobster leftovers into a yummy bisque.

How to Make Sure Your Seafood is Fresh

- **Shellfish:** if your shellfish is raw then make sure it is alive when you buy it. Shellfish are highly susceptible to bacterial contamination and should be kept alive until cooked. Give them a shake to see if they move; sometimes they can get sleepy so it's best to wake them up!

- **Fishy odor:** this is the first giveaway that your fish isn't fresh. Fresh fish should only have a mild smell and it's not a horrid one.

- **Whole fish** should have nice, shiny, and bulgy eyes, never cloudy or sunken in. Fish should look wet all over, never slimy.

- **Fish skin** should look tight—never cracked or dry—and almost have a bounce to it.

- **Mussels:** when you buy mussels they should all be tightly closed. If any are open, give them a sharp tap and they should close up.

- **Scallops** are similar to mussels; if you are buying them in the shell, make sure either the shells are closed or that they close when you tap them. Often you will buy them out of their shells and that's fine, just make sure they look and smell fresh and have a bright color. The main body should be slightly translucent and clean looking and the roe a lovely orange/coral color.

Kitchen Tips

Butter
We always use full-fat, salted butter in our recipes. Neither of us understands the use of unsalted butter, even in a cake recipe. Salt brings out all the flavors!

Oil
We use vegetable or rapeseed or canola oil for most of our frying. Rapeseed or canola oil has the highest cooking heat so that's what we use in our fryers and frying things at a high heat. Look for the best quality oil you can find.

Eggs
We only use free-range eggs. Please try to avoid using battery eggs, all you need to do is google battery farms and it will put you off for life.

Milk
We mainly use whole milk in our dishes since it just has more flavor, but unless it's specified in the recipe don't worry if you only have 1% or 2% in the fridge—that will work just fine too.

Spices
In the Shack we throw in a pinch of this and a dash of that, so it's been a tough job converting things into exact measurements for this book. Follow your own tastes; if you don't like cumin, you don't need to put it in; if you like things spicy, add some more chili. We believe things should be altered to your personal taste; after all, we're all different.

Bouillon cubes
If you have time to make stock then well done you, that's amazing and just can't be beaten. We've written our recipes using bouillon cubes though since we understand most people don't have the time to make stock. It really doesn't make a difference what brand you use, but we like Knorr vegetable bouillon cubes. It's hard to get hold of a good fish stock since not many seem to capture that fishy taste.

Herbs
We use fresh herbs in everything—you don't want to ruin a nice bit of fish with dried herbs. And it may seem obvious but make sure you actually like the taste of a herb before you flavor your fishcakes with it! We often use dill but not everyone likes it, so just swap it for something you do like.

Cooking times
Every oven is different, everything cooks at different times, and fish fillets can be fat one day and thin the next. Don't go with the approach of "throw it in and take it out in 20 minutes and it will be perfect"—always check things as they cook, allow time for extra cooking, and be patient if your quiche is taking 45 minutes instead of 30.

Deep frying

We deep fry things like tempura battered fish and crab cakes—it's a quick and reliable way to cook fish all the way through keeping it crispy and tender. We use fryers in the Shack but it's simple to use a pan as an alternative. Don't be afraid of deep frying but do be very careful—a hot pan of oil isn't something to have on in the house with kids running around so always keep it at the back of the stovetop.

Slowly bring the temperature of your oil to a max of 375°F (190° C), then lower the heat and keep it low (the oil will stay hot). If you don't have a food thermometer, just drop in a piece of bread every now and then—if it sizzles you know it's hot enough.

"So, on a typical day, first of all I'd be up in the morning, probably about half past five or something like that, buying the fish at Peterhead. I'll get it delivered up to Inverness in the afternoon, and I'll bring it back here to deal with it. It's literally as fresh as can be, but if I'm buying it locally you're getting it fresher, you're getting it directly. The majority of our fish we buy local: our haddock and our cod we buy from the east coast, but the likes of our halibut, hake, turbot, monkfish we buy local here and our prawns and lobsters are local. Our scallops come from Shetland. Our mussels are rope-grown and come from the Western Isles. About 70% of the fish we get comes straight off the boat, and about 30% we buy from the market at Peterhead. We fillet the majority of the fish, myself and my father—we go at it, you know?

In April we get west coast haddock because the east coast haddock have spawned so there's no eating them then. After they lay their eggs they go really skinny, and it can take up to two months for them to come back again. They always say on the east coast they need the May water, so you'll not get a decent haddock until May comes in, after they've spawned. They're later spawning on the west coast. It's probably just as well because you then wouldn't get a decent haddock if they all spawned at the same time, you know? It's not even that they're not in good condition: there's no taste to them, they're peely-wally, they're just not good at all. Haddock is the most popular fish we sell; I'd prefer haddock to cod myself. Cod's more an English thing.

There's a lot more demand for fish these days than there was. In the past you could basically buy and sell all you wanted. Now I can buy as much as I want, but a fisherman can't sell as much as he wants—I can't buy any fish without putting a sales note through the fisheries office.

Before, there were quotas but nothing was getting recorded—that's why your boats used to land through the night in little harbors and all that kind of stuff, so they could land what they wanted and there was no record of it, you know? In 2005, when those buyers' and sellers' sales notes came in, the fishermen thought that was them finished because they weren't going to be able to land black fish. But actually it had the adverse effect because it put the price through the roof, so it worked out better for them. All the prices of our products have pretty much doubled since we first started.

People will still pay for quality. When I started 20 years ago, I used to buy a stone of haddock for £22 and sell it for £44 or something like that, but now I buy a stone of haddock for £52 and sell it for £58, so you need to sell a lot of fish to make your money. I'm probably pretty lucky because a lot of my fish doesn't have to go through a middleman. I get them directly off the boats; that's my only saving grace.

It's very seasonal; it's a feast or famine. You have to make your money in that five, six month period because in the winter time there's nothing like. I'm just lucky because I've got other businesses I can half fall back on; I wouldn't want to rely on fish totally."

Stephen Couper
Fishmonger

CHAPTER 1

White Fish

If the fishing is good...
go now. Tomorrow will
be too late.

White Fish

At the Shack we serve a selection of white fish dishes. It's hard to do pan-fried fish and whole fish even though we'd love to; being a takeaway service people are only happy waiting a certain amount of time and things have to be dished up pretty quick, so our menu reflects this. But we still have a lot of options: from a cod paella and monkfish curry to Thai-style fishcakes or the super-popular haddock wrap, we've managed to create many yummy fish dishes that work in the Shack. We never use frozen produce and this is particularly important with white fish, since you just can't quite get the same taste and texture with a frozen piece of haddock as you can with a fresh one. For us, putting in smaller fish orders more often with our fishmonger works best and people really notice our fish isn't frozen—so important since it's obviously not the cheapest option.

White fish spawn in February and March so won't be the best quality then since they can be a bit thin and tasteless. There's an old saying that white fish need May's month of water for the meat to really come on.

Different fish have very different textures: some are delicate and flaky while others are more solid and meaty. So it's always good to know how your fish will change when it's cooked. For example, it's easy to tell if haddock is cooked: you push it apart and the meat should flake away, and it will be white and opaque. Fish like monkfish is a bit trickier: it's very meaty and won't flake apart but should be white and opaque inside when cooked. It can become rubbery if overcooked, so although it's a meaty fish it is also delicate to cook.

White fish can be kept in the fridge for three to five days if you've bought it straight from the fisherman. If bought from a shop or fishmonger, it will keep for more like two to three days so always check what the packaging says.

Haddock Wrap with Lemon Mayo and Pesto

This is by far our most popular dish. Perfect for people who aren't huge seafood lovers, it's the Shack's version of fish and chips. At first our friends and family would get annoyed with us if this wasn't on the menu, now everyone does. Safe to say it's now always on the menu!

Serves 4

Ingredients

4 fresh haddock fillets
   (approx. 1 lb 12 oz/800 g in total)
scant ½ cup (50 g) all-
   purpose flour
4 flour tortillas
pesto (page 229)
4 handfuls of mixed salad greens
sliced veggies, to serve (we use
   cucumber, red bell pepper,
   tomato, and red onion)
salt and black pepper

for the tempura batter:
1¼ cups (150 g) all-purpose flour
¾ cup (100 g) cornstarch
2 tsp baking powder

for the lemon mayo:
4 heaped tbsp mayonnaise
juice and zest of ½ lemon

vegetable oil, for deep frying

Check the haddock fillets for obvious bones by running your fingers down the sides and middle of the fillets—small bones will disintegrate when you cook the fish.

To make your batter, add the 1¼ cups (150 g) all-purpose flour, cornstarch, and baking powder to a bowl. Using an electric mixer or whisk, slowly beat in about 1¼ cups (300 ml) cold water until your batter is a thick but runny consistency. It should stick to your finger when you dip it in and there should be no lumps. Season the batter well with salt and pepper.

For the lemon mayonnaise, just mix the mayonnaise, lemon juice, and zest together until smooth, then season to taste.

Heat about 2¾ in (7 cm) vegetable oil to 350°F (180°C) in a large pan or deep fryer—the oil needs to be deep enough to submerge at least one fillet of haddock. Put the scant ½ cup (50 g) all-purpose flour in a bowl and dip a piece of fish first in the flour, then in the batter, making sure it is completely coated. Place carefully into the hot oil (giving the pan a gentle shake, so it doesn't stick to the bottom) and cook for around four minutes or until the batter is a light golden brown and crispy. Only fry one or two fillets at a time depending on the size of your fryer or pan—if they touch in the oil they will stick together. Remove and drain on some paper towels to soak up any oil. Repeat with the remaining fish.

To assemble, put a tortilla on the table and spread it with pesto and lemon mayonnaise. Add a handful of salad greens and a few slices of cucumber, tomato, red pepper, and onion—or whatever else you fancy—and then place your fish on top. Season, wrap, and enjoy!

Fish Finger Sandwich

If you have your peas and tartare sauce made beforehand, then this is a great thing to knock out for a quick dinner. You don't need to use haddock, any white fish will do, just make sure you adjust the cooking time according to how thick it is.

Serves 4

Ingredients

2 large fillets of haddock
  (approx. 1 lb/450g in total)
scant ½ cup (50 g) all-
  purpose flour
2 large eggs, beaten
8 slices of good quality bread
tartare sauce (page 225)
salad for garnishing
vegetable oil, for deep frying
salt and black pepper

for the breadcrumbs:

3 slices of white bread
handful of fresh herbs, finely
  chopped (we use parsley and dill)

for the minty peas:

1½ cups (400 g) frozen petits pois
  (petite green peas)
handful of mint leaves
1 tbsp lemon juice

TIP: Use good quality peas in your minty pea purée as this makes all the difference with taste.

First, make your breadcrumbs. Simply put the bread and chopped herbs into a food processor and process until you have fine crumbs. Divide each haddock fillet into four equal strips so you have eight small fillets altogether. Put your flour in a bowl, your beaten eggs in another, and your breadcrumbs in a third, and season each bowl. Dip your haddock strips into the flour, then the eggs, and then the breadcrumbs, making sure you coat them completely at each stage. Lay your now breadcrumbed strips out on a plate and set aside.

Put a pot of boiling water on to cook your peas. When it's boiling add your peas and cook for three minutes until just tender—it's very important you don't overcook them or they'll lose their bright green color and fresh taste. Drain the peas and let them steam-dry for a minute, then pop them in your food processor with your mint, lemon juice, and salt and pepper. Process until you have a course purée.

When you're nearly ready to eat, heat the vegetable oil to 350°F (180°C) in a large pot or deep fryer. You must have enough room in your pot to submerge at least one strip of haddock. Carefully slide a few of your strips at a time into the hot oil and make sure they don't stick together by giving the fryer/pot a shake or mixing them with a metal spoon. Fry for two to three minutes until they are golden brown; haddock is a thin fish so it really doesn't take long to cook. Drain on some paper towels and repeat with the remaining fish. Toast the bread slices in a toaster or under the broiler and then you can assemble your sandwich! We spread on some minty pea purée, top with a couple of fish strips, then some tartare sauce, and a handful of salad. Serve with some red cabbage slaw (page 202) alongside.

Haddock Fishcakes

Fishcakes can often be a little bit bland and tasteless: you don't want to overpower your fish, but you also don't want to feel like you're just eating fish and potatoes! Add some smoked fish if you want a stronger flavor, but if you want to keep it light and fresh, don't be shy with your lemon, herbs, and seasoning.

Serves 4

Ingredients

14 oz (400 g) white potatoes, peeled
1 lb 2 oz (500 g) fresh haddock fillets
generous 2 cups (500 ml) whole milk
3 bay leaves
1 fish bouillon cube
½ bunch of scallions, sliced
2 garlic cloves, crushed and thinly sliced
½ red chili pepper, deseeded and thinly sliced
small handful of flat-leaf parsley, chopped
small handful of chives, chopped
juice and zest of ½ lemon
2 cups (250 g) all-purpose flour
2 eggs, beaten
salt and black pepper

for the breadcrumbs:
3 slices of white bread
small handful of fresh herbs, chopped (we use parsley and dill)

vegetable oil, for deep frying

Chop your potatoes into large chunks and put them in a pot with enough cold water to cover them. Add two pinches of salt, bring to a boil, and then simmer until soft. Drain and let them steam-dry.

While your potatoes are cooking, place your fish in a large sauté pan or frying pan, cover with milk, and add your bay leaves and some black pepper. Simmer your fish very gently until it flakes apart, making sure it doesn't boil since the milk can separate easily. Drain your fish in a colander over the sink, pushing the fish down to squeeze out as much liquid as possible. Throw out the bay leaves and flake the fish into a bowl (removing any stray bones).

Put your bouillon cube in a small mug, add two tablespoons of boiling water, and mix until you have a runny paste. Scrape this paste into the flaked fish and add the scallions, garlic, chili pepper, parsley, chives, and the lemon juice and zest. Mix well. When the potatoes are completely dry, mash them until there are no lumps, then add to the fish mix. Taste and season well.

To make the breadcrumbs, put the bread and herbs into a food processor and process until you have fine textured breadcrumbs.

Place your flour in one bowl, beaten eggs in another, and breadcrumbs in another and season each bowl. Roll the fish mix into eight evenly sized balls, then dip each one into the flour, then the egg, and then the breadcrumbs, making sure they are fully coated. Place them on a plate or baking pan.

TIP: Always taste your mix before you form the fishcakes so you can adjust the flavors before it's too late.

TIP: These fishcakes can be frozen for up to three months—it's easiest to wrap them individually in plastic wrap first.

We deep fry ours but they are just as good pan-fried if you prefer. To deep fry, put enough vegetable oil into a large pan or deep fryer to a depth that will fully cover a fishcake: don't overfill the pan since the oil will bubble up when the fish cakes are added. Heat slowly to 350°F (180°C), then carefully add a few fishcakes. Use tongs with your first cake and make sure the oil sizzles as soon as you put it in; remove it and wait if it doesn't. Fry until the fishcakes are golden brown and start to float in the oil—about five minutes. Remove carefully with a slotted metal spoon and drain on paper towels. Put in a warmed oven while you cook the rest of the fishcakes. If you are pan-frying, heat plenty of vegetable oil in a large frying pan—your fishcakes will soak up the oil and burn if there isn't enough. We flatten our fishcakes slightly since it makes them easier to cook. Fry them for around five minutes on each side, until crispy and golden brown all over.

Diego's Paella

This dish came from Diego, the Italian chef who worked for us in 2018. He would make this in a huuuge pan and always put the same amount of love into it. It always drew in the customers, but maybe the complimentary glass of sangria helped?

Serves 4

Ingredients

16 langoustines (about 2 lb/ 900 g), or substitute shell-on jumbo shrimp

2 good dashes of olive or canola oil

4 garlic cloves, finely chopped

2 red onions, diced small

1 red chili pepper, chopped

2 red bell peppers, 1 sliced, 1 diced

1 yellow bell pepper, diced

large handful of cherry tomatoes, halved

large handful of green beans, trimmed

2 tsp smoked paprika

small pinch of saffron threads

5¼ oz (150 g) Spanish dry- or semi-cured chorizo, chopped

1 fish bouillon cube

4¼ cups (1 liter) boiling water

zest of ½ lemon

1¼ cups (250 g) short-grain paella rice

1 lb 5 oz (600 g) skinless cod fillets, cut into ¾ in (2 cm) chunks

lemon wedges, to serve

salt and black pepper

TIP: You can use lots of different seafood in this recipe: sometimes we keep it simple and only use cod, sometimes we add mussels or squid.

Bring a pot three-quarters full of very salty water to a boil, then put in your langoustines. Cook for two to three minutes only (they will continue to cook in the paella), then dunk them straight into cold water, drain, and leave to one side.

Put a nonstick frying pan or wok over medium heat and warm up your oil. Add your garlic, onions, chili pepper, and diced bell peppers, and sweat for 10 minutes or so, turning the heat down and adding a splash more oil if your veggies start to burn.

Add your sliced red peppers, cherry tomatoes, green beans, and paprika, and season with pepper. Increase the heat and add your saffron and chorizo. While this is cooking, crumble your bouillon cube into the boiling water and stir until it has dissolved.

Once your veggies are nice and caramelized, pour in about half of the stock and the lemon zest. Now add your rice, give the whole mixture a good stir, and bring up to a simmer. Paella rice will take around 20 minutes to cook; it will soak up the stock as it cooks so turn down the heat when it starts to thicken up and keep adding more stock as you go along, trying not to mix your rice too much. Add your cod chunks and langoustines halfway through. When your rice still has a slight bite, it is nearly ready, so turn your temperature right down and add a little more stock if you think it needs it. When the rice is tender, serve with a wedge of lemon (and a glass of sangria).

Breaded Cod Wrap with Curried Mayo and Red Cabbage Slaw

Cod is a totally underrated fish in Scotland, which we don't understand; it is a lovely meaty fish that can stand up to strong flavors without being lost—just make sure you season it really well. It goes beautifully with the curried mayonnaise and red slaw.

Serves 4

Ingredients
4 fresh cod fillets
¾ cup (100 g) all-purpose flour
2 eggs, beaten
4 flour tortillas
curried mayo (page 225)
red cabbage slaw (page 202)
4¼ oz (120 g) mixed salad greens

for the breadcrumbs:
4 slices white bread
small handful of fresh herbs, finely
  chopped (we use parsley and dill)
zest of 1 lemon
salt and black pepper

vegetable oil, for deep frying

TIP: If you want to check if your fillets are cooked, open them up in the thickest part. If the fillet breaks away, it is ready.

First, make your breadcrumbs. Simply add all the ingredients into a food processor and process until you have a fine crumbs.

If your cod is filleted to good portion sizes then you are good to go. If it is a full side of cod, fillet out the large bones—you will be able to feel them—and then slice it into two long, thin pieces. Cod is a much thicker fish than haddock, so we normally use two smaller fillets to make up one portion.

Now get three bowls and put your flour in one, your beaten eggs in another, and your breadcrumbs in the third. Season each bowl. Dip your cod fillets into the flour, then the eggs, and then the breadcrumbs, making sure they are completely covered at each stage or your egg won't stick to your flour, or your breadcrumbs to your egg, etc. Lay your now breadcrumbed fillets out on a plate.

Heat the vegetable oil to 350°F (180°C) in a large pot or deep fryer. Place one or two fillets carefully into the pot—you don't want them to touch in the oil or they will stick together. Give the pan a gentle shake, so nothing sticks to the bottom. Cook for three to five minutes until the breadcrumbs are golden brown and crispy (cooking time depends on how thick your fillets are but your fish should float when it is fully cooked). Drain on paper towels to soak up any oil. Repeat with each remaining fillet.

To assemble, spread a tortilla with the curried mayonnaise and a handful of red slaw. Add salad greens and then place your fish in the middle. Season, wrap, and enjoy!

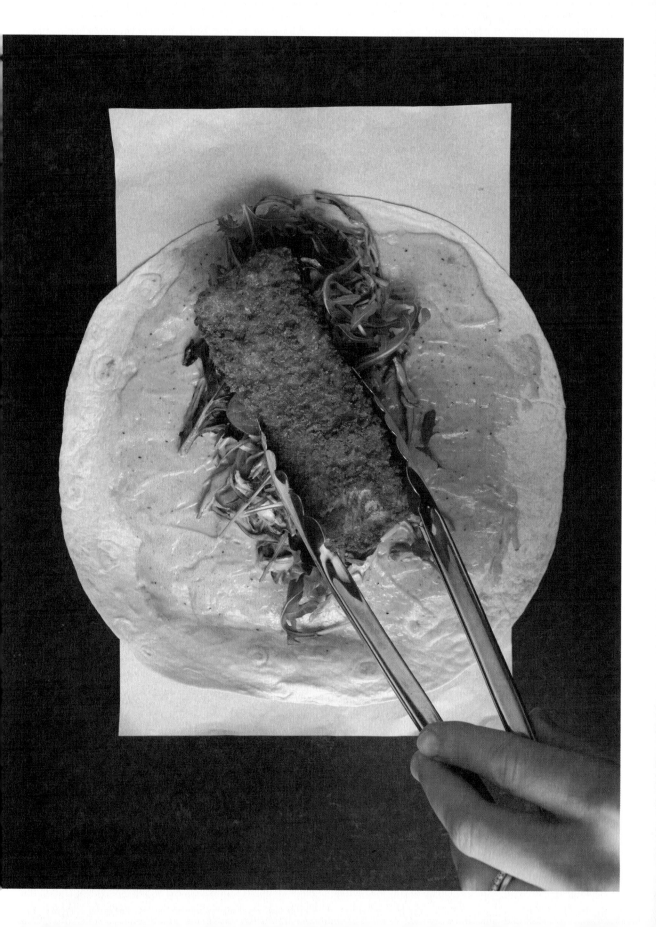

Cod and Chorizo Stew

This is a wonderful heartwarming stew; it just feels wholesome and comforting. The sour cream on top is, we think, really important and creates a lovely smooth finish. In the Shack, we always serve it with lemon and herb couscous (page 211) and it goes down a storm.

Serves 4

Ingredients
dash of vegetable or canola oil
3½ oz (100 g) Spanish dry-cured chorizo, halved and sliced into nice chunks
1 white onion, chopped
2 garlic cloves, finely chopped
1 red bell pepper, chopped
1 x 14 oz (400 g) can chickpeas, drained and rinsed
1 tbsp tomato paste
1 fish bouillon cube
1 tsp ground cumin
2 tsp smoked paprika
1 tsp cayenne pepper
1 tbsp honey
2 x 14 oz (400 g) cans chopped tomatoes
4 skinless cod fillets (1 lb 5 oz/600 g in total) cut into large chunks
4 handfuls of curly kale, sliced
salt and black pepper

to serve:
4 small pitas, toasted
4 tbsp sour cream
4 wedges lemon

TIP: This also freezes really well—freeze before you add the cod and kale.

Put your pot over medium heat and add the oil and chorizo. Cook until the chorizo releases its oil, then add in the onions, garlic, and red pepper. Cook these down for about five minutes until soft and sweet. Add the drained chickpeas, tomato paste, the crumbled bouillon cube, cumin, smoked paprika, cayenne, and honey and fry for another five minutes. Stir in the canned tomatoes and simmer for 15 minutes more. Taste and season with salt and pepper.

Heat a large frying pan over medium heat and add a splash of oil. Get the pan nice and hot and put in your cod pieces, then season with salt and pepper. You want to sear the fish until it is only just cooked. Add your tomato and chorizo stew to the pan along with the kale and simmer for another five minutes, until the cod flakes apart and the kale is tender. Serve with toasted pita, sour cream, and a wedge of lemon, and a big pile of lemon and herb couscous on the side.

Pan-Fried Cod with Pesto and Breadcrumb Topping

If you have some pesto in the fridge, then why not mix it with some breadcrumbs to create this great topping? With some added Parmesan and lemon zest it brings out all the flavors in the cod and turns a potentially dull meal into something simple yet delicious. Serve it up with some creamy mashed potatoes.

Serves 4

Ingredients

2 slices of white bread
juice and zest of ½ lemon
1 cup (100 g) grated Parmesan
2 tbsp basil or red pepper pesto
  (page 229)
4 cod fillets (skin left on)
dash of vegetable or canola oil
3½ tbsp (50 g) salted butter
salt and black pepper

Preheat your oven to 350°F (180°C). Pulse the bread in a food processor until you have coarse breadcrumbs, then mix in the lemon zest, Parmesan, and pesto and season with salt and pepper to taste.

Using your fingers, check the cod for bones and season the skin of the fish. Heat a frying pan and add the oil. Once the pan is hot, put in your fish, skin side down, season, and cook for two minutes or until the skin is crispy. Turn over, add your butter and lemon juice to the pan, and cook for another two minutes. Flip your fillets back over so they are skin side down and spoon a quarter of the breadcrumb pesto mixture on top of each one. Transfer the fish to a baking dish and cook in the oven for eight minutes. The timing will depend on the thickness of your fillet, so to check if they are cooked, push a knife in to see that the flesh flakes apart and is white and opaque.

TIP: When pan-frying fish with skin on, we always dry the skin first since this helps it to get extra crispy.

Thai-Style Cod Fishcakes

We love Thai food, but with the local produce we have it's not often we get to spice things up. This is a great way to jazz up fishcakes with some more interesting flavors.

Serves 4

Ingredients

14 oz (400 g) white potatoes
1 lb 2 oz (500 g) cod fillets
generous 2 cups (500 ml) whole
  milk
2 bay leaves
1 stick of lemongrass (give it
  a bash with the blunt side of
  your knife)
1 fish bouillon cube
1 tbsp boiling water
3 scallions, sliced
1 small red chili pepper
1 garlic clove, crushed
handful of fresh parsley
handful of fresh cilantro
1 tbsp Thai red curry paste
juice and zest of 1 lime
scant ½ cup (50 g) all-
  purpose flour
2 eggs, beaten
salt and black pepper

for the breadcrumbs:
3 slices of white bread
zest of 1 lime

vegetable oil, for deep frying

Peel and chop your potatoes into large chunks, then put them in a pot and cover with cold water. Add two pinches of salt, bring to a boil, and simmer until soft. Drain and let them steam-dry.

While your potatoes are cooking, place the cod into a large sauté or frying pan, and cover with milk. Add your bay leaves, lemongrass, and some salt and pepper and simmer very gently until the fish flakes apart. Make sure the milk doesn't boil since it can separate very easily. Drain the fish in a colander over the sink, making sure you push the fish down to squeeze out as much liquid as possible. Throw out the bay leaves and lemongrass.

Put your bouillon cube in a small mug and dissolve it in a tablespoon of boiling water to get a runny paste. Add the paste into the drained potatoes and mash. Once you've got rid of all the lumps, mix in your fish, scallions, chili pepper, garlic, parsley, cilantro, curry paste, lime juice, and zest. Mix it all together until everything is completely combined, then taste for a good balance of flavors and add more of anything—chili, lime, herbs—you'd like.

Put the bread in a food processor and process until you have fine textured crumbs. Stir in the lime zest. Place your flour in one bowl, beaten eggs in another, and breadcrumbs in a third, and season each bowl with salt and pepper. Roll the fishcakes into eight balls, and dip them into the flour, then the eggs, and then the breadcrumbs. Make sure the fishcakes are fully coated at each point.

TIP: To freeze, individually wrap the breadcrumbed, uncooked fishcakes and defrost fully before frying.

We deep fry our fishcakes but you can easily pan-fry them if you prefer. If you are deep frying then heat the vegetable oil to 350°F (180°C) in a large pot or deep fryer—you need enough oil to fully submerge at least one fishcake. Carefully drop a couple of fishcakes into the oil and fry until the breadcrumbs are crispy and golden brown and the fishcakes start to float—around five minutes. Remove with a slotted metal spoon and drain on paper towels. Repeat with the remaining fishcakes. If you are pan-frying them, heat plenty of vegetable oil and fry your fishcakes for around five minutes on each side until they are crispy and golden brown all over—we usually flatten them a bit to speed up the cooking time.

Fish Pie

Just a feel-good family dinner! You can use any fish you like—we like to use a mix of haddock and cod—just try to stick to the same proportions of fresh fish to smoked. In the Shack, we always use lemon, caper, and dill butter (page 227) instead of plain butter to fry the vegetables—it makes it extra delicious so give it a try if you have some in the fridge.

Serves 4

Ingredients
for the mash:

2 lb (900 g) white potatoes, peeled
1¾ tbsp (25 g) salted butter
⅔ cup (150 ml) whole milk
1 egg
3 scallions, chopped
salt and black pepper

for the filling:

3½ tbsp (50 g) butter or lemon, caper, and dill butter (page 227)
dash of canola or vegetable oil
1 onion, chopped
6 scallions, chopped
2 garlic cloves, finely chopped
2 carrots, chopped
1 red bell pepper, thinly sliced
scant ½ cup (50 g) all-purpose flour
1 fish bouillon cube
2½ cups (600 ml) whole milk
1 lb 2 oz (500 g) mixed fish fillets, cut into ¾ in (2 cm) chunks
7 oz (200 g) cold-smoked haddock, cut into ¾ in (2 cm) chunks (or substitute other smoked fish)
1 bay leaf
1 tbsp wholegrain mustard
handful of parsley, chopped
splash of heavy cream (optional)
4 eggs
Cheddar cheese (optional)
salt and black pepper

Preheat your oven to 350°F (180°C). Put your potatoes in a large saucepan and cover with cold water. Add a good pinch of salt, bring to a boil, and cook until the potatoes are soft. Drain in a colander and let them steam-dry.

While your potatoes are cooking, make a start on the filling. Melt the butter and oil in a pot over medium heat, then add your onion, scallions, garlic, carrots, and red pepper. Season with salt and pepper and sweat for around 10 minutes. Stir in the flour and the crumbled bouillon cube and cook for another five minutes or so. Slowly pour in the milk and keep stirring until you have a smooth consistency, then add the fish, bay leaf, and mustard. Turn the heat to low and simmer until the fish is just starting to break apart, then stir in the parsley and a splash of heavy cream if you're using it. Take off the heat.

Now back to your mash! Add the butter, milk, and one egg to the potatoes and mash until there are no lumps left, then mix in the chopped scallions and season to taste. Boil the remaining four eggs in a small saucepan for around seven minutes. Drain and leave to cool, then peel and cut them into quarters.

To assemble the pie, pour the fish filling into a large oven dish and arrange the eggs evenly on top, then spoon on your mashed potatoes, spreading it out into an even layer. If you would like, grate a bit of Cheddar cheese on top. Your fish pie can be made ahead to this point. When you're ready to eat, bake for around 30 minutes until it is hot in the middle and golden brown on top—we like to put it under the broiler for a couple of minutes at the end to crisp up the potatoes.

TIP: Don't have your oven too hot or the sauce can split.

TIP: Fish pie freezes really well, just cover in plastic wrap once assembled.

Pan-Fried Halibut with Lemon and Dill Sauce

Halibut is a very gently flavored fish so it works really well with this creamy but zingy lemon sauce. With some crushed baby potatoes and a big pile of sweet roasted veggies, this is a delicious, super quick and easy dinner.

Serves 4

Ingredients

a splash of vegetable
  or canola oil
4 skinless halibut fillets
  (approx. 5¼ oz/150 g each)
3½ tbsp (50 g) salted butter
1 garlic clove, finely chopped
⅔ cup (150 ml) heavy cream
juice of ½ lemon
½ tsp English mustard
small handful of fresh dill, chopped
salt and black pepper

Put a frying pan over high heat and add a splash of oil. Run your fingers along the halibut fillets to check for bones.

Once the pan is hot, place the halibut fillets in and season. Don't move them around the pan, just leave them to cook for a couple of minutes. Once the halibut starts to brown on the bottom, flip over, season, and turn the heat down to medium. Cook for another two or three minutes. Add the butter and garlic to the pan and let it foam up before stirring in the cream, lemon juice, mustard, and dill. Simmer for three to four minutes, basting the fish with the sauce until it is cooked—check by pushing a knife into a fillet to check that it's white and opaque in the center.

Creamy Hake Risotto with Roasted Butternut Squash

This is probably one of Kirsty's favorite dishes in the Shack. It goes really well with a big arugula salad with balsamic dressing (page 231). We always fry the vegetables in our basil pesto butter (page 227) but you can use plain butter if that's what you have.

Serves 4

Ingredients

1 butternut squash, cut into
    ½ in (1 cm) cubes
dash of canola oil
1 tsp ground cumin
1 tsp smoked paprika
2 strips of bacon
3½ tbsp (50 g) butter or basil
    pesto butter (page 227)
2 garlic cloves, peeled and finely
    chopped
4 large shallots (or 8 small ones),
    finely sliced
1 red chili pepper, finely sliced
1 large leek, sliced
1½ cups (300 g) arborio rice
sprig of thyme
scant ½ cup (100 ml) white wine
1 vegetable bouillon cube
1 fish bouillon cube
4¼ cups (1 liter) boiling water
1 lb 2 oz (500 g) hake, filleted,
    skinned, and chopped into
    1½ in (4 cm) chunks
¾ cup (200 g) frozen petits pois
    (petite green peas)
8 asparagus spears, cut into
    1½ in (4 cm) lengths
small handful of parsley, finely
    chopped
juice and zest of ½ lemon
Parmesan shavings
salt and black pepper

Preheat your oven to 425°F (220°C). Put the butternut squash on a baking pan, drizzle with a dash of oil, and sprinkle over the cumin, smoked paprika, and some salt and black pepper. Roast in the oven for about 30 minutes until soft, turning every now and then. Turn the heat down a bit if it starts to burn.

Put your frying pan over medium heat and add the bacon. Cook until crispy on both sides, remove from the pan, and leave to drain on paper towels, then roughly chop when it is cold. Add the butter and a little more oil to the bacon fat left in the pan, and when it's melted add the garlic, shallots, chili pepper, and leek and sweat for around 10 minutes. Now add your arborio rice and fry for another five minutes. Add the thyme sprig, pour in the white wine, and cook, stirring, until it is absorbed by the rice. Dissolve the bouillon cubes in the boiling water and add a generous ¾ cup (200 ml) to the risotto. Once it is absorbed, add another generous ¾ cup (200 ml), and repeat until the risotto is creamy but the rice still has a little bit of bite. This will take about 20 minutes. You may not need to use all your stock, or you may want to add more water at the end.

Stir in the hake, peas, and asparagus and add the roasted butternut squash. Simmer on low heat for around 10 minutes, adding more water if it looks too thick. Finish off with the finely chopped parsley and lemon juice and zest, and season to taste, then scatter each serving with the chopped bacon and some shavings of Parmesan.

TIP: Always trim your asparagus by breaking off the ends at the first point they easily snap. They all snap at different lengths!

How to fillet a monkfish tail

Quite often monkfish is sold as a tail, so it's quite useful to know how to fillet one. A filleting knife is the best knife to use but if you don't have one just use the sharpest one in the kitchen.

First place the monkfish on your chopping board and remove the skin, pulling it from the top of the monkfish down towards the tail. It helps to push your thumb in between the skin and meat to help separate it and you can also use your knife to help. Remove the flaps on either side of the monkfish and trim off any more excess skin. Now pull as much sinew as you can away from the top to the bottom of the tail.

To remove the monkfish meat from the spine, turn your monkfish so that the spine is facing upwards, then score the meat as close as possible to the spine from top to bottom. Once you are happy that you've scored it as close as possible, cut your first fillet away along one of score lines, keeping your knife tight to the spine. Flip your fish on its side so the spine is now flat on your chopping board and cut your second fillet off, again keeping your knife as close to the spine as possible. We recommend slicing it so the knife is cutting away from you.

Now tidy up the fillets, removing any leftover sinew or skin. It can be hard to remove all of the sinew so don't worry too much if there's some left—you can end up getting a bit carried away and start losing some meat. You now have two large fillets that are ready to be used.

TIP: Monkfish is a bottom feeder and therefore often has small worms in the meat. Don't worry too much if you see any—they are harmless. Just pick them out with the tip of your knife.

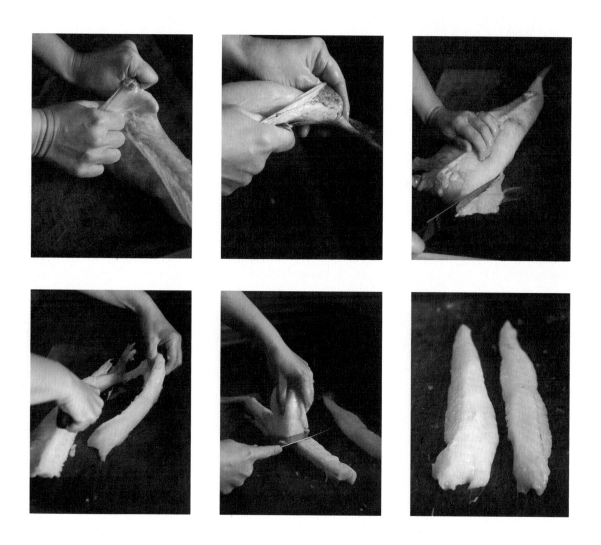

Tempura
Monkfish Bites

Monkfish bites are so popular in the shack we could have them on every day, but our fryers wouldn't cope! We serve them up on some beet couscous (page 211) with curried mayonnaise (page 225) to dip them in.

Serves 4

Ingredients
1 lb 2 oz (500 g) monkfish fillets
scant ½ cup (50 g) all-purpose
flour

for the tempura batter:
1¼ cups (150 g) all-purpose flour
¾ cup (100 g) cornstarch
2 tsp baking powder
salt and black pepper

vegetable oil, for deep frying

To make your batter, place the 1¼ cups (150 g) all-purpose flour, cornstarch, and baking powder in a bowl, and season well. Using a electric mixer or whisk, slowly add about 1¼ cups (300 ml) water, mixing all the time—you want your batter to be a thick but runny consistency. It should stick to your finger when you dip it in and there should be no lumps.

Carefully heat the vegetable oil to 350°F (180°C) in a large pot or deep fryer. With a sharp knife, cut your monkfish fillets into 1½ in (4 cm) chunks. Toss them in the all-purpose flour, then dip into the batter and drop them into your hot oil, being careful not to touch the oil with your fingers (you can use tongs). Make sure you have enough room in the pot to move your monkfish bites around with a metal spoon, since they will stick together or to the bottom if you don't. Cook for around three minutes until they are light brown. Remove with a slotted metal spoon and place on paper towels to drain.

TIP: Monkfish must never be served undercooked as it can make you ill. Cut one of your bites in half to check it's cooked—it should be a white and opaque. It is a very meaty fish so it won't flake apart.

Thai-Style Monkfish Curry

This is one of our favorite curries to make both in the Shack and at home. Monkfish is a great fish to use in curries because it is meaty and holds its own in the strong flavors.

Serves 4

Ingredients

1 lb 2 oz (500 g) monkfish fillets
2 tbsp vegetable or canola oil
2 red onions, roughly chopped
1 white onion, sliced
1 red or green chili pepper, thinly sliced (and deseeded if you don't like it too hot)
3 garlic cloves, finely chopped
½ in (1 cm) piece ginger, peeled and finely chopped or grated
2 red bell peppers, thinly sliced
2 tbsp Thai red curry paste
2 tbsp tomato paste
1 tsp cayenne pepper
2 tsp ground cumin
2 tsp smoked paprika
1 fish bouillon cube
2 tbsp runny honey
2 x 14 oz (400 g) cans chopped tomatoes
1 x 14 oz (400 ml) can coconut milk
2 tbsp Thai fish sauce
2 tbsp sweet chili sauce
2 tbsp soy sauce
1 lime, quartered
1 tbsp vegetable or canola oil
salt

to serve:

4 pitas, toasted
4 tbsp crème frâiche
handful of snap peas, sliced diagonally
4 scallions, sliced

Cut the monkfish into 1½ in (4 cm) chunks and set aside for now. Put a pot over medium heat, and add the oil, red and white onions, chili pepper, garlic, ginger, and peppers. Sweat everything down until your onions are caramelized—we normally do this for at least 10 minutes. When everything is very soft and sweet, stir in your red curry paste, tomato paste, cayenne pepper, cumin, smoked paprika, and the crumbled bouillon cube, and then add the honey. Cook this for five minutes until the smell of the spices really comes through, stirring all the time. Add your canned tomatoes, coconut milk, fish sauce, sweet chili sauce, and soy sauce. Squeeze and add in the quartered lime. You now want to cook this at a low simmer for about 15 to 20 minutes to thicken up your sauce and make it taste super delicious. Add a bit of salt if it needs it and keep stirring every five minutes to stop it burning on the bottom.

You can add the monkfish straight to the curry, but we like to pan-fry it first to seal it. Get a nonstick frying pan and put in about a tablespoon of oil.

Get the oil super hot and then fry your monkfish until it's slightly browned all over; you're not trying to cook it so don't worry if it's still raw in the middle. Add your monkfish to your curry, and simmer very gently for another five minutes until it's just cooked through (don't overdo it or it can get very rubbery).

Serve with a big pile of wild rice to soak up the sauce, some toasted pita, a spoonful of crème frâiche, and some crunchy snap peas and scallions to finish it off.

TIP: If you want to freeze this, freeze just before you add the monkfish.

"I started fishing in 1970. When I left school I was studying navigation with the intention of going into the Merchant Navy, and I just threw all that up and decided I was going to go into the fishing.

It was mainly prawn [shrimp] creel fishing for the first 14 years. We had a boat, the *Brighter Morn*—she was a 40-foot boat and we worked her at the creels. In 1978 we converted her to enable us to go to the trawl, especially in wintertime. Traditionally everybody used to take their creels all ashore from about November time to February, because when the herring boats came here a lot of them would fish for herring in the lochs. So you lost a lot of gear getting towed away. It gave the ground a rest, it gave you a chance to get your gear all sorted out for the spring fishing— which traditionally was the best time of year to catch prawns. So that's what we started to do, and then when they took the three-mile limit off in '85, we were rigged all ready for the trawl. We mended all the creels that winter with the intention of going to the creels in the spring, but we were making more money trawling and it was an easier life. So we then went trawling full time. We mainly worked in the loch dodging Russian klondykers—the fishing was good but we did a heck of a lot of damage to the trawl gear as the klondykers weren't exactly environmentally friendly with a lot of rubbish just getting heaved over the side of their ships.

Trawling and creel fishing—both have their moments. There's a bit of ground out there in the loch, just a narrow bit like a plateau on top of the bank. I used to fish it with the creels and you'd get a fishing out of it, maybe 12 kilos a day if you were lucky. But I've trawled in there in the summertime and got something like 700 or 800 kilos of live prawns and 250 kilos of tails, so if you multiply the tails by three to give a whole prawn weight that equates to another 750 kilos of whole prawns. It astounded me: the prawns must have been just knee deep, you know? And we used to catch prawns in the trawl where you'd never ever catch prawns with the creels. It was bizarre.

I've always preferred trawling. Creeling is hard work; it's very, very monotonous, because you're just on the same ground all the time. When we first started you could up your gear and move places. But as more creelmen got into it, it became that once you'd got your little bit of ground you were stuck there. With trawling I enjoyed it more because I could go places, I wasn't just stuck in the same bit of ground all the time. Creels were like that back in the 70s.

When I was with Roy on the *Harvest Lily* we could just look at a piece of ground and say, 'Och well, nobody's been there for six months; we'll go and put a few fleets over there and try that.' You can't do that now.

When I started fishing first there was no live or no heads on, everything was tailed. And the prawns were bigger. It must have been '72 when we started landing live prawns. Our buyer was putting them mainly to Spain and was probably one of the first to put stuff out there. Now 90% goes to Spain, maybe even more than that. They know what to do with a prawn. People here don't know what to do with it. You can give them a lobster and they'll eat the tail and leave the claws, the head and everything else. But if you give one to an Italian or a Spaniard, they'll spend two hours sucking the life out of it, eating everything.

We've got the best fishing grounds in Europe and if you look west of the Hebrides out on the edge of the continental shelf, it's all Spanish boats—Spanish, Russian, French, all trawling, gillnetting, or longlining. We've had a few of the Scottish pelagic boats fishing out there but there's a huge fleet of Russian boats, Faroese boats, Norwegians—they traditionally have fished there but you wonder how there's any pelagic fish left out there. Inside the 12 mile limit they can't come, but we have got the best grounds and we should look after them. We've sold a lot of our quota to foreign boats, who are registered under the British flag but have Spanish crews and contribute very little to our economy. The fish all go back to Spain on Spanish lorries [trucks] who even bring their own food stores in from Spain.

Your fishing licence is worth more than your boat. I don't think they issue new licences now so I suppose as boats get old you're sitting with a boat that's worth nothing and a licence that might be worth £100,000. In some of the cases, some of the pelagic ones, you're looking at licences that are worth millions just for a piece of paper that you were given. It makes it hard to get into the industry now. Unless your father's got a boat, it's very hard for a young boy to leave school and say, 'I just want to be a fisherman.' When I started it was dead easy.

It's hard to sell it to young people. You're saying, 'Well, look, you're going to have to get up at 4 o'clock in the morning; you'll probably be working 12-14 hours a day. Sometimes—a lot of times—you won't make enough money.' If you work out what you earn per hour it's pretty abysmal, but it's a love of the job. When I sold my last boat I thought that was it, but it wasn't long before I had to push a dinghy into the sea.

I just wanted to be on the water. But when you're standing on deck and it's a poor, poor day and you're getting lashed and you haven't had anything to eat for whatever it is and the creels are coming up and are getting blown over or the trawl's coming up and it's torn and you've got to mend it, you think, 'God, there's got to be better jobs than this.'

We used to have some wild sessions just drifting around. You went alongside guys at sea and you had a wee dram and a yarn. Nowadays guys are working thousands of creels with hardly enough time to have a cup of tea.

I love herring in oatmeal. I would eat that all day. When I first came to Ullapool the first guy I ever met was Harry MacRae. His uncle used to push dinghies out from the beach and hire them out, and his wife would always cook herring in oatmeal. Just a dry frying pan, a little oil, then she used to dip them in milk and then put the oatmeal on. Myself and Harry, we would sit and eat a dozen between us. Or even a dozen each. Hard job now to get a dozen herring for your supper!"

John Britten
Skipper of MFV *Brighter Morn* and MFV *Intrepid*

Wind from the west, fish bite the best. Wind from the east, fish bite the least. Wind from the north, do not go forth. Wind from the South blows bait in their mouth.

CHAPTER 2

Smoked Fish

Smoked Fish

When you smoke a fish you completely change it, turning it from something delicate and mild tasting to a strong and intense ingredient. In some dishes it works really well and in some not so much. We tend to always use smoked fish in soups; you can lose the flavor of fresh fish in a soup and a lovely cullen skink has got be made with smoked fish—it's the saltiness and smokiness that makes the dish what it is. But on the other hand, we wouldn't want a fillet of smoked cod slapped in front of us for dinner. Some people love it and would have smoked everything, so it really is personal preference. Smoked fish can be great in fish cakes as it intensifies the flavor, and it's so yummy in pâtés where the taste of the fish bursts through the smooth, bland cream cheese.

Smoked fish has a much longer shelf life that fresh fish and can be kept in the fridge for up to three weeks if it's vacuum packed. If it's not vacuum packed, we would keep it for up to a week. It's also better to freeze than fresh fish as keeps its structure better when it defrosts and you don't lose much flavor.

You can smoke pretty much anything, so if you are someone who loves smoked fish then why not think about buying your own smoker? It's such a fun thing to play around with and, if you don't want to buy one, do some research in making your own since they're pretty simple to knock up yourself.

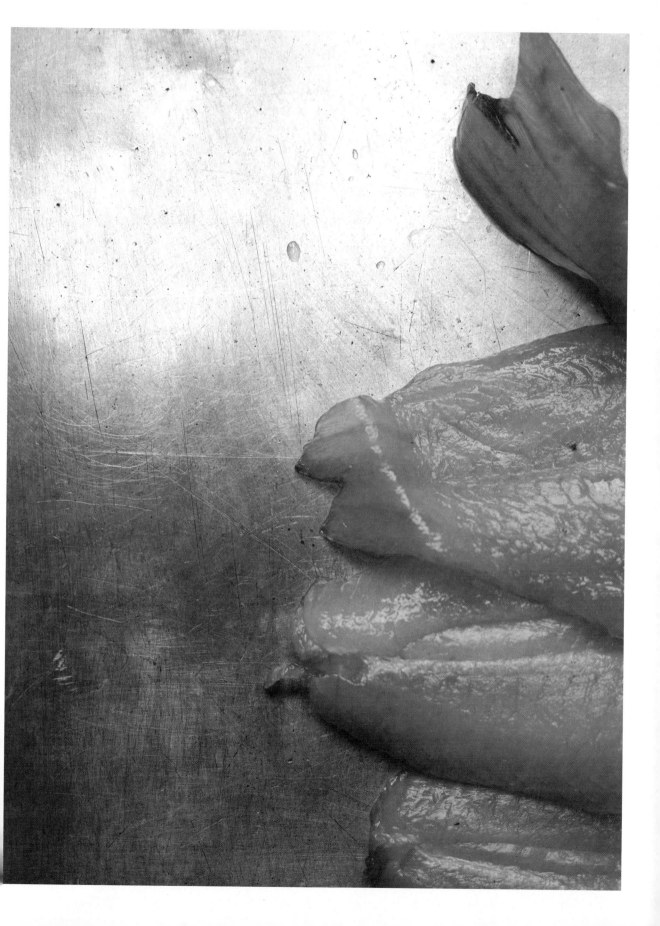

Spicy Smoked Fish Soup

This one is a recipe Kirsty made in the Shack by literally throwing some of her favorite ingredients into a pot, and now we get complaints if we take it off the menu. It's one of the locals' favorites, and all those warming spices make it a great soup for winter.

Serves 4–6

Ingredients

1¾ tbsp (25 g) salted butter

dash of vegetable or canola oil

2 red onions, finely diced

2 white onions, thinly sliced

2 celery sticks, thinly sliced

2 red or yellow bell peppers, thinly sliced

1 carrot, cut into quarters lengthways and sliced

1 red chili pepper, deseeded and thinly sliced

2 garlic cloves, finely chopped

3 large potatoes, peeled, quartered and sliced

juice of 1 lemon

1 fish bouillon cube

1 tbsp tomato paste

2 bay leaves

2 tsp paprika

2 tsp ground cumin

2 tsp cayenne pepper

2 tsp garam masala

2 tsp medium curry powder

5 dashes Tabasco sauce

4 fillets undyed cold-smoked haddock (2 lb/900 g in total), or substitute fresh haddock

⅔ cup (150 ml) heavy cream

salt and black pepper

Heat the butter and oil in your soup pot over medium heat. Add your red and white onions, celery, peppers, carrots, chili pepper, and garlic and sweat for around 10 minutes, stirring all the time, to bring out all the delicious, sweet flavors. Add your potatoes and lemon juice and sweat for a further 10 minutes. This is when the bottom of your pot starts to get sticky and then burned so keep stirring every now and then.

Crumble in your fish bouillon cube, then add the tomato paste, bay leaves, paprika, cumin, cayenne pepper, garam masala, and curry powder. Season with plenty of black pepper and five generous dashes of Tabasco. Sweat for a further five to 10 minutes—it will smell amazing and it pays to be patient to give the spices time to release all their flavors into the veggies—then pour in enough boiling water to cover and simmer until your potatoes are soft.

Check your haddock fillets for any bones, then add them to your soup with the cream. Simmer over low heat until your fish is cooked—it will fall apart—and your soup is lovely and thick. Taste and add seasoning.

TIP: This is a good one for the freezer. Freeze before you add in the fish, then just defrost, reheat, and throw in the haddock and cream.

TIP: Adjust the spices to whatever suits your personal taste.

Cullen Skink

We make HUGE pot-loads of Cullen Skink at the shack and in mid-season we can get through three pots within hours. By the last few portions the soup is so lovely and thick a spoon sticks upright in it, and these pots of goodness are always requested by locals.

Serves 6–8

Ingredients

3½ tbsp (50 g) salted butter

1 tbsp vegetable or canola oil

3 white onions, diced

1 celery stick, diced

2 leeks, diced

1 bay leaf

juice of ½ lemon

5 dashes Tabasco sauce

1 fish bouillon cube, crumbled

1 lb 12 oz (800 g) white potatoes

4 fillets undyed cold-smoked
   haddock (2 lb/900 g in total),
   or substitute fresh haddock

generous 2 cups (500 ml) heavy
   cream (or as much as you want!)

salt and black pepper

Heat the butter and oil in your soup pot (adding the oil stops the butter from burning). Stir in the onions, celery, and leeks and sweat for around 10 minutes. The longer you cook it down, the sweeter and tastier your soup will be, just remember to keep stirring so nothing sticks to the bottom. Add the bay leaf, lemon juice, Tabasco, and plenty of black pepper and crumble in the fish bouillon cube, then sweat down for another five minutes.

Peel and dice the potatoes: we like to leave them nice and chunky; it gives the cullen skink a good texture. Cook them with the veggies for another five to 10 minutes to help release the starch to make a good thick soup. Now add about 4¼ cups (1 liter) of water so all the vegetables are completely covered and simmer over medium heat until the potatoes are cooked. Add a little more water if too much evaporates.

Check the haddock fillets for any bones, then add them to the pot. Reduce the heat to low and cook until the fish breaks up. Pour in the cream and taste to see if you need more salt or pepper. You can serve it now, or if you like you can simmer away for another 10 minutes over very low heat to thicken your soup even more.

TIP: Cullen skink can be frozen for up to three months. Just put it in a freezer-safe container once the potatoes are cooked but before you've added the fish.

Thai-Style Smoked Haddock Noodle Soup

This is a great soup, light and fresh from the lemongrass but really substantial and filling as well. It goes perfectly with toasted pita bread.

Serves 4–6

Ingredients

1 tbsp vegetable or canola oil

2 white onions, chopped

2 red peppers, finely sliced

1 garlic clove, finely chopped

½ in (1 cm) piece fresh ginger, peeled and grated

1 red chili pepper, deseeded and chopped

1 tbsp Thai red curry paste (or more if you like it hot)

1 tbsp tomato paste

1 fish bouillon cube, crumbled

4 lime leaves

1 lemongrass stalk (give it a bash with the blunt end of your knife)

1 lime, cut in half

a glug of fish sauce

a glug of soy sauce

6⅓ cups (1.5 liters) boiling water

3 scallions, sliced

5¼ oz (150 g) rice noodles

4 small fillets undyed cold-smoked haddock (1 lb 12 oz/800 g in total), or substitute fresh haddock

1 x 14 oz (400 ml) can coconut milk

small handful of cilantro, chopped

black pepper

TIP: The soup freezes really well. Just freeze before you add the rice noodles and smoked haddock.

Put your pot over medium heat and add the oil, onions, red pepper, garlic, ginger, chili pepper, curry paste, and tomato paste, then turn the heat to low and cook until the onions have softened, 10–15 minutes. Crumble in the fish bouillon cube and add the lime leaves, lemongrass, lime halves, fish sauce, soy sauce, and most of the scallions (leave some for a garnish). Give it a hefty grind of black pepper and cook for another five minutes to release the flavors.

Pour the boiling water into the pot and simmer until the vegetables are soft. Increase the heat to medium. Put in the rice noodles, cover, and cook for a couple of minutes until the noodles are just slightly softened. Check the smoked haddock fillets for bones and then add them, whole, to the pot, along with the coconut milk and cilantro. Simmer until the fish is cooked and the noodles are tender. Finish off with the remaining chopped scallions.

Smoked Mackerel Pâté

Kirsty's sister Katie works in the Shack, and she gave this recipe a tweak by adding a cheeky scoop of mayonnaise (she LOVES mayonnaise!). She has perfected it and she's now always the one who makes the mackerel pâté. For a change we sometimes make this with hot smoked trout—as seen in the photo—and with a really smoky bit of trout, it is absolutely scrummy. Both are perfect for wee canapés, and they make a great side dish to take on your picnic.

Serves 4

Ingredients

3 hot-smoked mackerel fillets (9 oz/250 g in total)
generous 1 cup (275 g) full-fat cream cheese
1 tbsp mayonnaise
juice and zest of ½ lemon
2 scallions, chopped
5 or 6 chives, chopped
a few sprigs of curly parsley, chopped
black pepper

Put the smoked mackerel fillets on a chopping board skin side up. Slowly peel the skin off the meat, then turn the fillets over and remove the middle section of bones: you'll see there's a darker section running down the middle of the fillet, so run your fingers along it and you will feel a line of small bones. Use a knife to cut either side of them, and discard the bones. You will now be left with two sides of the fillet. Flake these into a large mixing bowl, checking for any stray bones—they're very small so can easily be missed.

Add the cream cheese, mayonnaise, lemon juice and zest, scallions, chives, and parsley and season really well with black pepper. Give it a good mix until you have a smooth texture.

Variation: Smoked Trout Pâté

Use 9 oz (250 g) hot-smoked trout instead of the smoked mackerel fillets, leave out the scallions, and swap the parsley for a finely chopped sprig of dill.

TIP: This can be kept in the fridge for up to five days—it's even more delicious the day after you make it. It's perfect for freezing too.

Smoked Haddock Fritters

Fritters are one of our favorite things to eat anyway, so we thought why not make some fishy ones and make them even more delicious! Fenella's boys go mad for these. If you want to make this dish extra special, serve it with some fresh salsa and guacamole.

Serves 4

Ingredients

4 fillets undyed cold-smoked
   haddock (2 lb/900 g in total),
   or substitute fresh haddock or
   smoked trout
2 handfuls of frozen petits pois
   (petite green peas)
1⅓ cups (200 g) canned or frozen
   corn kernels (drained if canned)
3 scallions, thinly sliced
7 oz (200 g) zucchini, grated and
   squeezed to get the moisture out
1 tsp smoked paprika
juice of ½ lemon
1¼ cups (150 g) self-rising flour
8 eggs
4 tbsp canola oil
4 tbsp sour cream
a good squeeze of sweet
   chili sauce
black pepper

Check your smoked haddock fillets for bones, then chop into small chunks. Place your peas in a colander and run under warm water until thawed, then set aside to drain. In a large bowl, combine the the corn, scallions, zucchini, smoked paprika, lemon juice, flour, and plenty of black pepper. Beat four of the eggs and add to the bowl, and give the mixture a good stir. Add the smoked haddock and peas and mix again.

Put your frying pan over medium heat and add the canola oil (you want enough oil to shallow-fry the fritters; you can always add more between batches). Spoon dollops of the mixture into the pan—we make our fritters about 4 in (10 cm) in diameter. Fry for three minutes, then turn the fritters over and cook for another three minutes, until golden brown on both sides. Fry them in batches depending on the size of your pan and put them in the oven set to about 285°F (140°C) to keep them warm.

While the fritters are cooking, it's time to poach your remaining four eggs. Give your eggs a good rinse under cold water first. Bring a saucepan of water to a simmer. Put the eggs—with the shell still on—into the water and cook for 20 seconds, then get them out with a slotted spoon. This seals the eggs inside and makes poaching much easier! Crack the eggs into the water, making sure you hold them as close to the water as possible when you do it because if you drop them from a height they will come apart. The fresher the eggs the firmer they will be when poached. Poach the eggs for three or four minutes; the cooking time depends on the size of your eggs, so to check that they're ready lift one out and give it a wee shake—you want the yolk to wobble but the egg white to be firm. Once they're done, put them on some paper towels or a dish towel to dry off. Mix the sour cream with a good squeeze of sweet chili sauce. Serve the fritters in a stack topped with a poached egg, and drizzle with the creamy sauce. Delicious!

Smoked Haddock and Kale Hash

Fenella came up with this recipe and now we both constantly make it for dinner—SO yum! You can use any smoked fish you like.

Serves 4

Ingredients

2¼ lb (1 kg) baby potatoes
1¾ tbsp (25 g) salted butter
2 garlic cloves, finely chopped
1 white onion, diced
1 fish bouillon cube
1⅓ cups (200 g) canned or frozen
  corn (drained if canned)
2 tbsp canola or vegetable oil
2 large fillets undyed cold-smoked
  haddock (1 lb 2 oz/500 g in
  total), chopped into chunks (or
  substitute fresh haddock)
5¼ oz (150 g) curly kale, shredded
4 free-range eggs, shells
  cleaned well
small handful of parsley, chopped
salt and black pepper

for the crème frâiche sauce:
⅔ cup (150 ml) crème frâiche
1 tbsp lemon juice
3 or 4 chives, chopped

Pop the baby potatoes in a large pot with enough cold water to cover and a good pinch of salt and boil until they're just cooked. Drain and let them steam-dry. While your potatoes are cooking, put a high sided frying pan over medium heat, add in the butter, garlic, and onion, and fry until everything is soft—around 10 minutes. Crumble in the bouillon cube, then add the corn and fry for another 10 minutes.

Cut your cooked potatoes into halves or quarters, depending how big they are. Pop a frying pan over high heat, then add your oil and let it get super hot. Throw in your potatoes (you want them to sizzle with the heat) and season well with salt and pepper. Fry them for 15 to 20 minutes until they get nice and crispy. They can sometimes start to stick to the bottom of the pan, so watch you don't burn them and keep moving them around. Once you are happy with the potatoes, add in the fried corn-onion mix, the haddock, and the curly kale and cook until the kale is tender and the haddock is starting to flake. Make your sauce: just mix together the crème frâiche, lemon juice, and chives, and season to taste.

Finally, boil a saucepan of water to poach the eggs. Once the water is boiling, turn down the heat and put all four eggs—with the shells still on—into the water and cook for 20 seconds, then get them out with a slotted spoon. This seals the eggs inside and makes poaching much easier! Crack the eggs into the water, making sure you hold them as close to the water as possible when you do it because if you drop them from a height they will come apart. The fresher the eggs the firmer they will be when poached. Poach the eggs for three to four minutes; the cooking time depends on the size of your eggs, so to check they're ready lift one out and give it a wee shake—you want the yolk to wobble but the egg white to be firm. Place the poached eggs on some paper towels or a dish towel to dry off.

Serve the hash with a poached egg on top and a dollop of the crème frâiche sauce beside it. Sprinkle with parsley and salt and lots of black pepper.

Curried Smoked Haddock Scotch Eggs

There's nothing more satisfying than cutting into this Scotch egg and watching its runny yolk oozing out. Don't worry if you don't get the egg quite right the first time—just try and try again!

Makes 4

Ingredients

6 medium eggs
14 oz (400 g) white potatoes, peeled and cut into chunks
14 oz (400 g) cold-smoked haddock (or substitute fresh haddock)
generous 2 cups (500 ml) whole milk
3 bay leaves
1 fish bouillon cube
1 cup (150 g) canned or frozen corn kernels (drained if canned)
juice and zest of a lemon
3 scallions, sliced
small handful of parsley, chopped
small handful of chives, chopped
1 tbsp madras curry powder
1 tsp smoked paprika
1 tsp ground cumin
1 tsp garam masala
1¼ cups (150 g) all-purpose flour, plus extra if needed
vegetable oil, for deep frying
salt and black pepper

for the breadcrumbs:

·3 slices white bread
small handful of curly parsley, finely chopped

for the mayo:

3 tbsp mayonnaise
juice and zest of ½ lemon

Put a saucepan of water on to boil and, once boiling, drop in four of the eggs. You want to cook them for four minutes to keep them soft so when you cut the Scotch egg open it's still runny inside. Drain and submerge in cold water. Carefully peel the boiled eggs as soon as they're cool, and pop them in the fridge or freezer—getting them cool in the fridge really helps later, since it makes coating them much easier and prevents them bursting.

Put the potatoes in a saucepan and cover with cold water. Add a pinch or two of salt, bring to a boil, and simmer until soft. Drain and let them steam-dry, then mash, making sure there are no lumps.

While your potatoes are cooking put your haddock pieces in a large pot and cover with milk (don't worry if some haddock sticks out, you can push it back under). Add your bay leaves and some black pepper. Simmer the fish very gently until it flakes apart, but make sure it doesn't boil since the milk can separate very easily. Drain the fish in a colander over the sink, pushing the fish down to squeeze out all the liquid. Throw out the bay leaves and flake the fish into a large bowl, removing any bones you find.

Put your bouillon cube in a small mug and dissolve it in a couple of tablespoons of boiling water to get a runny paste. Add this to your flaked fish along with the corn, lemon juice and zest, scallions, parsley, chives, curry powder, smoked paprika, cumin, and garam masala. Mix it all together until it's completely combined, then taste and adjust the flavorings as you like. Add the fish mixture to your mashed potatoes and mix really well, then season to taste.

Now get your boiled eggs out of the fridge/freezer and roll them in all-purpose flour—this will help the coating stick to them. Cover your eggs with a thick layer of the fish mixture, making sure there are no holes or splits in it, and roll into a ball shape. Be very gentle while doing this since you can easily burst your eggs.

To make your breadcrumbs, put the bread and parsley in a food processor and process to fine crumbs. Beat the remaining two eggs. Put the breadcrumbs in one bowl, beaten eggs in another, and flour into a third and season each one. Dip the Scotch eggs into the all-purpose flour, then the eggs, and then the breadcrumbs, making sure they are fully covered at each stage with no cracks. Again, be very gentle when doing this so you don't burst the eggs.

Now to cook your Scotch eggs. Heat the oil in your deep fryer or pot to 300°F (150°C). Carefully place your Scotch eggs in the oil and cook until they start to float and the breadcrumbs go golden and crispy—this normally takes seven to eight minutes. Being very careful, since your oil will be very hot, remove them with a slotted metal spoon and drain on paper towels. You may need to fry them in batches, depending on the size of your pot—if you need to keep the cooked ones warm, just pop them on a baking pan in the oven at 300°F (150°C).

Mix the mayonnaise, lemon juice, and zest in a small bowl, and season to taste. Serve your perfectly soft-boiled Scotch eggs with a big dollop of lemon mayo and enjoy watching that runny yolk ooze out!

TIP: We use a deep fryer to fry these, but you can also use a large pot—just be careful and heat the oil up slowly to 300°F (150°C). You need to use enough oil to be able to submerge at least one Scotch egg but don't fill it too much since the oil will rise when you add your eggs.

TIP: These freeze really well once cooked—just let them get cold and wrap them individually.

Smoked Haddock, Pea, and Chorizo Macaroni and Cheese

If you feel like jazzing up your mac and cheese, try this. The smoked haddock and chorizo gives it an amazing smoky flavor and the peas freshen it up. A great way to get your kids to eat more fish! Smoked trout also works really well as an alternative to smoked haddock.

Serves 4

Ingredients

7 tbsp (100 g) salted butter
1 onion, finely chopped
1 garlic clove, finely chopped
½ red chili pepper, finely chopped
1 vegetable bouillon cube
3 heaped tbsp all-purpose flour
2½ cups (600 ml) whole milk
10½ oz (300 g) Cheddar
  cheese, grated
small handful of curly parsley,
  chopped
14 oz (400 g) macaroni
3½ oz (100 g) Spanish dry-cured
  chorizo, chopped into chunks
3 fillets undyed cold-smoked
  haddock (1 lb 5 oz/600 g in
  total), chopped into chunks (or
  substitute smoked trout)
1 cup (150 g) fresh or frozen peas
small handful of fresh chives,
  chopped
salt and black pepper

TIP: Cooking times can be different for different pasta brands so look at the package and take off two minutes from the suggested cooking time to make sure it doesn't overcook.

Put a large saucepan over medium heat and add the butter, onion, garlic, and chili, then let it all sweat off for a good eight to 10 minutes until everything is nice and soft and very sweet. Make sure you keep stirring so nothing burns. Crumble in the bouillon cube along with plenty of black pepper, and fry for another minute before adding the flour. Cook for a minute or two to make a roux, then slowly add the milk, whisking all the time since you don't want it to be lumpy. Cook over low heat until the sauce has thickened, then take it off the heat and add the grated cheese. Stir until the cheese has melted into the sauce, add your parsley, and season with salt and pepper.

Put a large pot filled with water over high heat and bring to a boil. Cook the macaroni for six to seven minutes—it will keep cooking after you drain it so you want it to be al dente—and drain in a colander. Heat a small frying pan and add the chopped chorizo—you don't need to add any oil since the chorizo will release plenty as it heats up. You want to get it nice and crispy so fry it for a few minutes over high heat, stirring and reducing the heat if it starts to burn. Keep a few pieces of chorizo aside to garnish your dish at the end. Add the smoked haddock and the peas to the remaining chorizo in the frying pan and cook until the haddock starts to flake. Stir the contents of the pan into the cheese sauce and mix in the pasta. You might need to give everything another quick blast of heat. Garnish with the reserved chorizo pieces and a sprinkle of chopped chives, and serve.

Pan-Fried Smoked Mackerel

This is so easy it doesn't really count as a recipe but we thought we'd add it in since people are always surprised at how delicious smoked mackerel is cooked. We serve it with crispy herb potatoes (page 214) and some fresh green salad with a sharp balsamic or basil dressing, and it always goes down a storm.

Serves 4

Ingredients
4 hot-smoked mackerel fillets
  (12 oz/350 g in total)
1 lemon, cut into quarters

Heat a frying pan over medium heat. Place the fillets of mackerel skin side down in the pan. Cook for around two minutes: the natural oils will start to release, and the skin will crisp up. Turn the fillets over and cook for another two minutes, making sure the fish doesn't burn. Smoked mackerel is already cooked so you are only heating it up—the cooking time may vary slightly depending on how fat a fillet you have.

Serve with a wedge of lemon and some herby crispy potatoes on the side.

Shack Quiches

We always make some quiches when we're having a buffet or any kind of large get-together, and they never last long. We use a 10 in (25 cm) cake pan to make a nice deep quiche with plenty of filling.

for the pastry crust
1½ cups (175 g) all-purpose flour
5 tbsp (75 g) butter
1 tsp smoked paprika
zest of 1 lemon
salt and black pepper

Preheat your oven to 400°F (200°C) and butter and flour a 10 in (25 cm) cake pan. In a food processor, mix your flour, butter, paprika, and lemon zest with some salt and pepper until they're all combined. Slowly add cold water, a tablespoon at a time, until your pastry just starts to clump together, then stop immediately—you don't want it to be too wet. On a floured worktop, roll the dough out until it's big enough to cover the bottom and sides of your cake pan, then smooth it into the pan so it completely lines the inside. Put in the fridge for 10 minutes.

Prick your pastry with a fork, then put a piece of parchment paper over the bottom and weigh it down with some pie weights. Cook for 20 minutes on the bottom shelf of your oven, then remove the pie weights and the paper and cook for another 10 minutes or until the pastry starts to brown.

cont.

TIP: Always let the quiche go cold before you cut it since it will fall apart if you do it when it's hot.

TIP: Make sure your fish is flaked or cut pretty small —if it's too chunky the quiche will be hard to slice.

TIP: If you don't have pie weights you can use rice or dried lentils.

Fillings

Smoked Trout
and Goat Cheese

serves 6–8

Ingredients
3½ tbsp (50 g) salted butter
glug of vegetable or canola oil
3 garlic cloves, peeled and finely chopped
4 red onions, thinly sliced
1 tbsp honey or brown sugar
2 tbsp balsamic vinegar
1 vegetable bouillon cube
6 eggs
scant ½ cup (100 ml) whole milk
generous ¾ cup (200 ml) heavy cream
a small handful of chives, chopped
3½ oz (100 g) hot-smoked trout, flaked
3½ oz (100 g) soft goat cheese, crumbled
a few sprigs of parsley, chopped
salt and black pepper

Preheat your oven to 350°F (180°C). Melt your butter and oil in a frying pan over high heat, then add your garlic and onions. Lower the heat and slowly fry them until they are dark and caramelized, which will take at least 20 minutes. When they are very soft and sweet, increase the heat and add your honey and balsamic vinegar along with your crumbled vegetable bouillon cube. Season with salt and pepper and cook for another 10 minutes until your onions become nice and sticky.

Whisk your eggs, milk, cream, and chives in a large bowl, and season well. Spread your caramelized onions over the bottom of your cooked pastry base, then pour in the egg mixture and scatter over your trout, goat cheese, and chopped parsley. Cook for about 30 minutes until your quiche starts to brown—it should still have a bit of wobble but be firm to touch.

Fillings

Smoked Haddock
and Tomato

serves 6–8

Ingredients
6 eggs
scant ½ cup (100 ml) whole milk
generous ¾ cup (200 ml) heavy cream
zest of 1 lemon
small handful of parsley and dill, chopped
3½ oz (100 g) mix of Cheddar and Parmesan, grated
2 handfuls of cherry tomatoes, halved
3½ oz (100 g) undyed cold-smoked haddock (or
  substitute fresh haddock), cut into small chunks

Preheat your oven to 350°F (180°C). While your pastry is cooking, whisk your eggs in a large bowl with the milk, cream, lemon zest, herbs, and half the cheese and tomatoes, and season well. Pour the egg mixture into your cooked pastry base and scatter with your smoked haddock and the remaining cheese, then arrange the rest of the tomatoes evenly on top. Cook for around 30 minutes, until your quiche starts to brown and is wobbly but firm to touch.

Quick and Easy Shack Baked Potatoes

Bored of your everyday baked tatties? Then these four simple and quick recipes for baked potato fillings are a great way to jazz them up and try something different. Red cabbage slaw (page 202) or some sweet roasted veg makes a great side.

To bake your potatoes

Preheat your oven to 300°F (150°C). Put your potatoes on a baking pan and prick with a fork all over. Rub the skins with olive oil, salt, and pepper—we use lots of salt as it makes the potato skins crispy and delicious. Bake for an hour and a half, turning over halfway through. Then bump up the heat to 400°F (200°C) and cook for another 30 minutes, giving them a good shake halfway through. If you want your skin to be super crispy, crank up the heat to 425°F (220°C) for a final 10 minute blast. Serve up with one of the following fillings.

Smoked Trout

serves 4

Ingredients
7 oz (200 g) hot-smoked trout, flaked
4 tbsp crème frâiche
juice of ½ lemon
small handful of chives, chopped
approx. 10 oz (280 g) red cabbage, sliced paper thin
2 tsp white wine vinegar
2 tsp sugar
salt and black pepper

Mix your trout, crème frâiche, lemon juice, and chives and season with pepper. In a separate bowl mix your cabbage with the vinegar and sugar and season well with salt and pepper. Fill your baked potato first with a spoonful of red cabbage and then pile in the smoked trout mixture.

Cont.

Baked Cod and Hollandaise

serves 4

Ingredients
4 cod fillets
1 lemon, quartered
4 sprigs of parsley
hollandaise sauce (page 221)
a small handful of chives, finely chopped

Put each piece of cod on a square of foil with a lemon wedge and a sprig of parsley on top and season well, then wrap up to make four sealed parcels. Pop in the oven with your baked potatoes for the last 20 minutes. Check the cod is cooked by pushing a fillet apart to see if it is white and flaky. Split your baked potatoes and put a piece of cod on each one, then pour over plenty of hollandaise sauce and scatter over some freshly chopped chives.

Sticky Langoustines

serves 4

Ingredients
32 langoustines (about 4 lb/1.7 kg),
  cooked and peeled (page 179),
  or substitute jumbo shrimp
juice of 2 limes, zest of 1
6 tbsp vegetable or canola oil
4 tbsp honey
4 tbsp sweet chili sauce
½ chili pepper, chopped
2 garlic cloves, crushed
1 heaped tsp sesame seeds
4 tbsp sour cream
salt and black pepper

Halve the langoustine tails and put them in a bowl. Mix with the lime juice and zest, oil, honey, sweet chili sauce, chili, garlic, and sesame seeds and season well. Once your potatoes are cooked, cook your langoustines in a frying pan over high heat until sticky and heated through, then serve on the baked potatoes with a dollop of sour cream on top.

Spiney and Cheese

serves 4

Ingredients
⅔ cup (160 g) crème frâiche
juice and zest of 1 lemon
a small handful of parsley, chopped
a small handful of chives, chopped
3½ tbsp (50 g) salted butter
2 garlic cloves, crushed
10 oz (280 g) peeled spineys (also called
  squat lobsters), or substitute shrimp
6½ oz (180 g) Cheddar cheese, grated
2 scallions, finely sliced
salt and black pepper

Mix your crème frâiche, lemon juice and zest, parsley, and chives in a bowl and leave in the fridge. Once your baked potatoes are ready, put a frying pan on to heat. Melt your butter with the garlic, then add your spineys, season well, and fry for a minute at most. Stir in the grated cheese until it starts to melt and pile into your baked potatoes. Top with a dollop of the crème frâiche mixture and a handful of sliced scallions.

CHAPTER 3

Molluscs

*The fishermen know
that the sea is dangerous
and the storm terrible,
but they have never found
these dangers sufficient
reason for remaining
ashore.*

I get my oysters from Guernsey Sea Farms. They've got a flooded quarry in Guernsey, they control the seawater coming in and out and they've got good bio security—they're miles from anywhere so you're reducing the risks of diseases from France or Ireland. They feed the tiny oysters an algae—when you see it, it's bizarre, they've got these huge vats of brown soup and it's specific algae that the oysters will do well on before they move on to bigger plankton. Then they get flown up and I pick them up in Inverness Airport.

I get something like 250,000 oysters in two boxes, sometimes a bit less. I get them at 7mm—you just pay more if you get a bigger size. They'll be very young at that size, probably six months old, max. So you've got a 7mm oyster and you get it into a bag with a 4mm mesh, and then that bag will probably need graded out at least once over that summer season.

They eat pretty much just plankton. They never starve but sometimes they'll certainly look thinner. The worst time is around January, February—there's very little plankton then. By the end of March it's kicking off again—it's to do with sunlight really, plankton; it's not as much to do with water temperature. Longer daylight hours, if we're lucky, sunshine, and you've got lots of nutrients in the water from over the winter. The weather has stirred up the bottom so there's loads of nutrients there and tons for the plankton to eat. Boom, it just takes off.

A good growth will be three years before I sell them. I used to grow bigger ones, but I think most people want an oyster at a certain weight. The most popular is a 65 gram, up to 75 or 80 grams. Some restaurants want a bigger one like a 90 or 100 gram-er. I just grill them if they're a bit too big.

The beauty of oyster farming is you're putting them out there and they get on with it, as long as there is plankton to eat. Plankton converted to delicious protein. It's using the sea, and it's not detrimental in any way, it's amazing. Mussels are even more amazing because you don't even have to buy the spat, you can just collect it from the wild and put them on ropes.

I've had hardly any problems with predators. Crab could be an issue when the oysters are small and the shells are thin but the bag mesh stops bigger crabs getting in. Mussel settlement in the bags can cause mortalities with their byssus thread which binds everything together. Despite their name I haven't had any problems with oystercatchers.

The oysters that are going to be sold, they're kept quite high up the beach so they come out of the water with every tide. The ones that are still growing are deeper so they come out of the water every second week in the spring tides. You want the ones you're selling to harden off a little bit and get used to being out of the water and staying shut. The recommended time you can keep an oyster out of the water before you eat them is seven days, but I've heard of people dropping them when they've been working on them and finding them three weeks later and they're still alive. I'm not sure I'd eat them though.

At home I would store oysters quite tightly packed so they're not spread out. Stack 'em up round and round and round on a circular dish and put a clean damp cloth on top so they stay damp. It's drying out that will kill them. Don't store them in water though, and make sure they're cup side down so they're sitting in their own juice.

I'm farming pacific oysters. When I started I was also growing native oysters which came from a hatchery. They're trickier in every regard. They grew at an incredibly slow rate and I had high mortalities. They just aren't as robust as the pacific oyster. Native oysters have a closed season because of spawning over the summer months. Pacific oysters don't spawn in Scottish waters because of the lower sea temperature but their taste does change and get more creamy as the sea temperature rises.

Loch Fyne Oysters had a pet oyster called Hamish, I'm sure that was over 25 years old, it was a monster of a thing. I have one from my first year that's escaped the shucking knife and it must be getting close to half a kilo. I should probably give it a name.

Joe Hayes
Ockran Oysters

Oysters

Well, oysters really aren't something for the fainthearted: slimy, slinky creatures that slither down your throat... I mean, that's one way to look at them. But that's not how our oysters often get described at the Shack.

We are so very lucky to have Joe who owns an oyster farm locally in Ullapool. His oysters get described as plump, creamy, silky, and above all delicious. We can take no credit for them at the Shack since all we do is shuck them, which does actually have some skill to it—but not enough to take any credit! Often we hear people say they are the yummiest oysters they've eaten and we both think a lot is down to the crystal-clear water they live in; after all they are filter fish.

Oysters tend to be good to eat all year round apart from February, when they can be too creamy. They can be kept up to one week in the fridge under good conditions—make sure they are kept cup-side down so the water doesn't leak out causing the oyster to dry out. You also want to keep a damp cloth over the top of the oysters to keep moisture in, or if you have some seaweed on hand that's even better.

How to Shuck Oysters

There's quite a knack to opening oysters, but once you have it you have it! Just make sure, if you don't have an actual oyster knife, that your knife tip is pointed but not sharp and is a good thickness so it won't snap. Our knife (see the photo) is really good.

Put a tea towel in the palm of your hand and the oyster on top, flat side facing upwards. Make sure the tea towel is covering your hand as it's very easy to slip with the knife.

Put the tip of the oyster knife into the narrow hinge end of the oyster, along the line where the two shells meet. Gently but firmly push the knife in and twist, opening up the shell, then slide your knife along, keeping it tight against the inside of the upper shell to cut the oyster where it connects to the shell.

Now you just need to cut the oyster from the bottom of the shell, keeping the knife as close to the shell as possible (you don't want to cut into the oyster meat at all). Flip the freed oyster upside down, check for any bits of shell, and eat immediately.

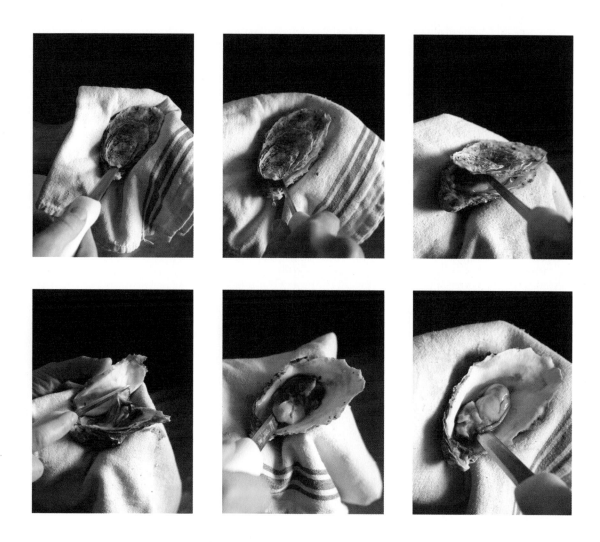

Oysters with Lemon and Tabasco

This is a simple way of serving oysters. Our oysters are so fresh and delicious, we often just serve them with this simple garnish at the Shack. The lemon just wakens up the taste buds while the Tabasco gives the oysters a good kick!

Ingredients

oysters, shucked (page 108)
lemon wedges
Tabasco sauce

Serve each oyster with a wedge of lemon and a few dashes of Tabasco—go easy since you don't want it to overpower the flavor of your oysters. Then squeeze over the lemon wedge and slurp the meat straight out of the shell. Down the hatch!

Deep-Fried Oysters

People usually love or hate oysters. Even if you are one of the haters, please try these since they are completely different to raw oysters. The tempura batter makes them lovely and crispy but the flesh stays moist and plump.

Serves 4

Ingredients
20 oysters, shucked (page 108)
scant ½ cup (50 g) all-purpose flour

for the tempura batter:
1¼ cups (150 g) all-purpose flour
¾ cup (100 g) cornstarch
2 tsp baking powder
salt and black pepper

for the mayonnaise:
scant 1 cup (200 g) mayonnaise
juice of ½ lemon
½ garlic clove, grated
½ tsp English mustard
salt and black pepper

vegetable oil, for deep frying

To make your tempura batter, put the all-purpose flour, cornstarch, and baking powder in a bowl and then, using a electric mixer or whisk, slowly add about 1¼ cups (300 ml) cold water, mixing all the time, until your batter is a thick but runny consistency. It should stick to your finger when you dip it in and there should be no lumps. Season the batter well with salt and pepper.

Mix all your mayonnaise ingredients together and season to taste.

Heat the vegetable oil to 350°F (180°C) in a large pot or deep fryer—if you are doing this in a pot, make sure to be careful and heat the oil slowly. It should be hot enough that a piece of bread dropped in will sizzle immediately.

Now coat each oyster in some flour and then dip it in the batter. Put a few at a time into your hot oil, being super careful of your fingers, and give them a good shake to ensure they don't stick together. Remove from the oil as soon as the batter is golden and crispy—no longer than three minutes. Drain on paper towels and serve immediately with your lemony, mustardy mayonnaise.

Buttered Oysters

An alternative way to cook oysters if you don't fancy them raw, this keeps their lovely fresh, delicate flavor but changes the texture. We serve them like this at the Shack and people who aren't usually keen on the idea of oysters seem much more inclined to try them.

Serves 4

Ingredients

3½ tbsp (50 g) salted butter
1 garlic clove, finely chopped
12 oysters, shucked (page 108)
small handful of curly parsley, chopped
1 lemon, quartered
salt and black pepper

First place your frying pan over medium heat, then add your butter and garlic and cook for five minutes, making sure your garlic doesn't burn.

Remove your oysters from the shells. Turn up the heat and toss in the oysters. Cook for around a minute over high heat, then add your parsley and season well with salt and pepper. Serve immediately straight from the pan, or sometimes we put them back in their shells with the buttery juices poured over. If you're doing that, heat the shells a bit in the oven first, which will help keep your oysters hotter for longer when you serve them.

TIP: If you're serving the oysters in the shell, the shell can be prone to tilting to one side. Stick them to the plate using something like a bit of leftover mashed potato or a blob of crème frâiche and that should stop them wobbling.

Mussels

Mussels are for some and not for others. Some people find the texture of them off-putting, but after they've been steaming away in a creamy, buttery sauce they soon start to get super delicious. The best part of a mussel dish always seems to be the same: that last bit of creamy sauce in the bottom of the bowl that gets soaked up with some warm crusty bread. The salty sea-ness from the mussels combined with your sauce always creates the perfect combination.

Our mussels are rope grown, since we find that they tend to be a lot less gritty than shore-picked mussels. Rope-growing mussels is a technique used by many mussel farmers in Scotland. In late spring, when mussels begin to spawn as the sea temperatures rise, the farmers drop old rope into the water, which is kept afloat by buoys. The larvae then naturally settle onto the rope surface and grow. It normally takes one to two years for them reach maturity.

There is a general rule that is super handy to go by when you're buying mussels: don't buy them in any month that has a R in it, since that's when there tend to be algae blooms in the water. Algae toxins can make humans really sick.

Mussels can be kept alive in the fridge for up to three days. A good rule of thumb is to make sure they are tightly closed and, if they're not, that they close up when you tap them. If you have one or two mussels that don't close, that's fine—just throw them away—but if a lot of them aren't closing it's a sign your mussels aren't very fresh anymore so it's probably worth getting rid of the lot.

Mussels don't need long to cook. They should always be tightly closed when you put them into your pan since this means they are alive—as soon as they start to open with the heat, start thinking about getting them off the stove. Always serve them up quick—cold mussels are never an appealing thought!

How to Clean Mussels

You'll need an oyster knife or another small but sturdy knife with a bit of bend to it.

When you're cleaning mussels, you want to remove any of the barnacles and the beard that comes out of the shell (which has a rope-like texture). We use the oyster knife since it's got a good thick edge—you don't want a sharp knife since you'll just ruin it and you need some force behind it to get rid of the barnacles.

Put the mussels in the sink and have the cold water running slowly. Hold a mussel in one hand and scrape the outside with the knife, getting rid of the barnacles and any other growths. The beard grows out of the middle of the hinge side of the mussel. Remove it by holding firmly with your thumb and forefinger and swiftly pulling upwards towards the tip of the mussel—don't pull outwards since this often means you don't pull it all out.

Once you have done them all, give them a quick rinse under cold water. Discard any that won't close their shells when you give them a tap, or any with cracked shells—they are dead and can make you sick. If you are keeping them to cook another day, place a damp tea towel over them and keep them in the fridge. This keeps the moisture inside the mussels.

TIP: Ask your fishmonger for rope-grown mussels if they can find them, since they tend to be less gritty.

Thai-Style Mussels

Plump mussels in a sweet, sour, spicy sauce—yum. If you don't like things too hot then you can take out the chili and use a gentler Thai curry paste; this will still be delicious and flavorful. Have some extra bread ready for the juices.

Serves 4

Ingredients

glug of vegetable oil

1 red onion, thinly sliced

1 red pepper, thinly sliced

1 garlic clove, finely chopped

½ chili pepper, deseeded and chopped

1 tbsp Thai red curry paste

½ vegetable bouillon cube

juice of 1 lime

4½ lb (2 kg) mussels, cleaned (page 117)

⅔ cup (150 ml) heavy cream

small handful of cilantro, chopped

good pinch of black pepper

Put a large saucepan over medium heat and add the oil, onion, red pepper, garlic and chili. Fry off until everything is lovely and soft—this usually takes around 10 minutes. Add the Thai paste, crumbled bouillon cube, and lime juice and fry off for another three to four minutes, until it smells fragrant and delicious.

Increase the heat, throw in the mussels, and put the lid on the pan. The juices from the veg and the water from the mussels will create steam and start to cook the mussels. Once the mussels are nearly all open (two or three minutes), turn the temperature down and add the heavy cream, cilantro, and black pepper. Slowly bring up the temperature until the sauce starts to bubble. Be careful when adding the cream as it can split if it's too hot. Once the mussels are all open, they are ready; don't leave them on the heat as they will overcook and go rubbery. Discard any that have stubbornly refused to open as they can make you sick.

Serve with a wedge of lime and crusty bread.

Mussels in a Creamy White Wine and Garlic Sauce

We think most people love the mussels mainly for the sauce, no? That's why we always make sure there's lots of it! And some chunky bread to soak it all up.

Serves 4

Ingredients

3½ tbsp (50 g) butter
1 white onion, diced
2 garlic cloves, chopped
½ vegetable bouillon cube
juice of ½ lemon
4½ lb (2 kg) mussels, cleaned (page 117)
1¼ cups (300 ml) white wine
generous ¾ cup (200 ml) heavy cream
small handful of curly parsley, chopped
plenty of black pepper

Put a large pot over medium heat and add the butter, onion, and garlic. Fry off for about 10 minutes until everything is lovely and soft. Crumble in the vegetable bouillon cube and add the lemon juice.

Increase the heat, throw in the mussels and the wine, and put the lid on the pot. The wine will make steam and start to cook the mussels. Once the mussels are nearly all open (two or three minutes), turn the temperature down to low and add the heavy cream, parsley, and black pepper. Slowly bring up the temperature until the sauce starts to bubble—be careful when adding the cream because if it's too hot it can split. Once the mussels are all open, they are ready—don't leave them on the heat or they will overcook and go rubbery. Discard any that stubbornly refuse to open.

Serve with a wedge of lemon and lots of crusty bread (not forgetting more butter).

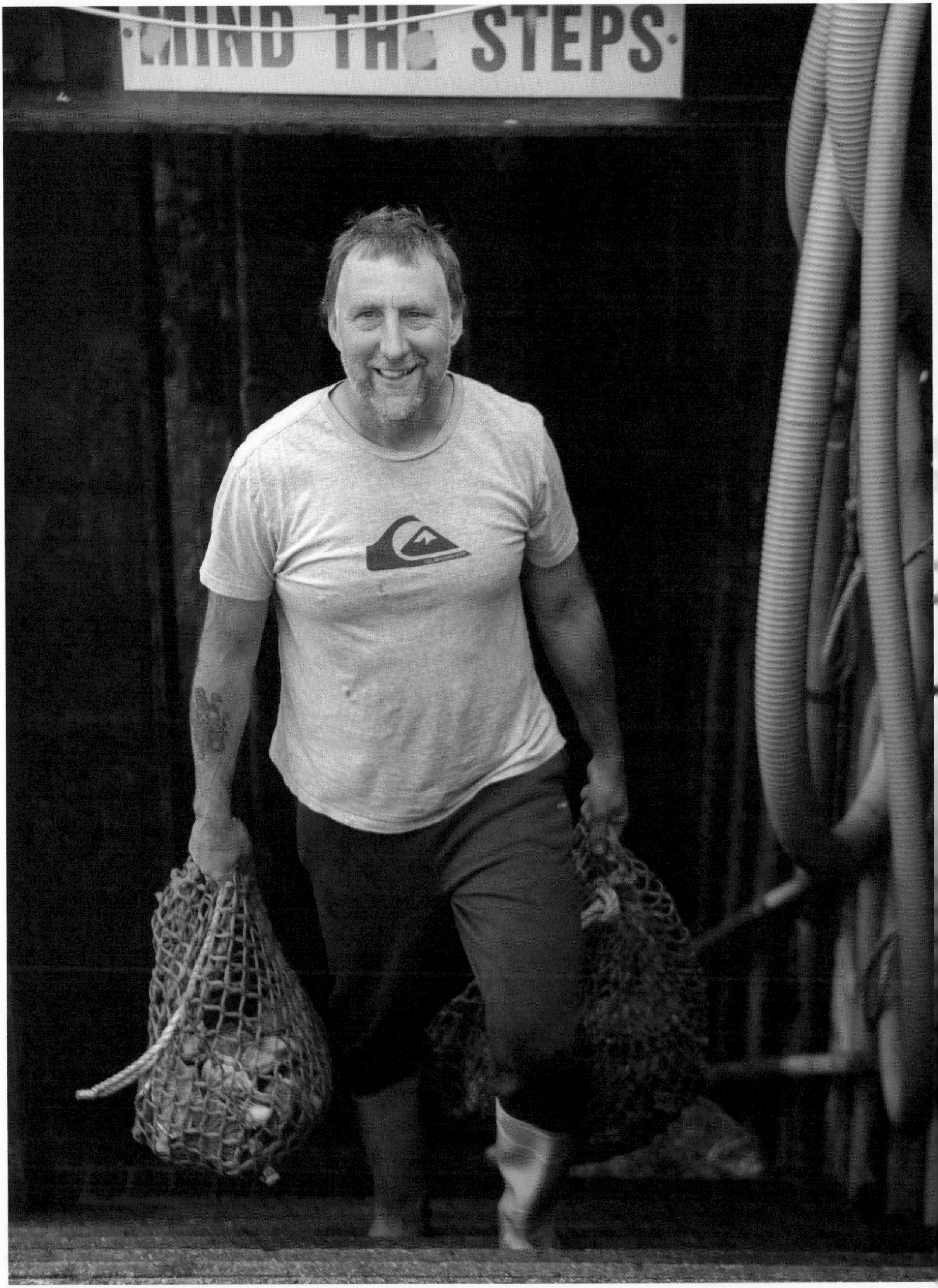
MIND THE STEPS

I fell into diving in the mid-80s after meeting a local scalloper by the name of Crazy Chris Howarth. Ullapool in those days had a fair few scalloping boats and the competition was generally friendly, but the real rivalry was with the large scallop dredgers. They tow heavy chain and tooth bars across the seabed and I've seen that first hand myself, the devastation that it causes to areas; it basically kills everything. It's horrendous what the dredgers do: they just wipe whole areas out of weed, any growth; not just scallops but crabs too.

People have become more aware of the damage they cause and areas are getting designated as Marine Protected Areas (MPAs) like we have here in the Summer Isles. What we're seeing here now is the crabs coming back into the sand where the dredgers used to go, and the whole place is becoming much livelier.

The scallops we gather are known as King Scallops or Pectin Maximus. They take around five years to reach table size. We use scuba diving equipment to catch the scallops, and we wear dry suits because of the water temperature—particularly in winter when it's down to five or six degrees [celsius]. We swim down with a couple of net bags, down to the bottom, and half way through our dive if we've got anything in the bag, we'll send it up on an inflatable buoy and the boat will pick that up. Then we'll continue on our dive until we're out of air or time, send up our other bag, and the boat will come along and just hang around for us.

We don't have a quota on what we can take out of the water —what limits our catch is just the amount of dive time that we can get. The more we dive, the nitrogen builds up in our bodies. It increases the risk of decompression sickness so you just can't dive every day of the week. It's physically demanding as well so it comes to a point where we just have to stop. Four or five days a week is plenty.

The dives are typically 40 minutes each but if we're down in the deep—35 meters—it might only be 20 minutes; and in the shallows, if we've got the daylight, it could be up to an hour. I'm a bit lazy as I've gotten older though...

We just keep fishing all year round. Obviously the summer is easier because the water temperature is much kinder to us and the weather is calmer. Winter gales cause us to lose a lot of days. But saying that, in the winter when we're going out we get frosty days and it's beautiful and flat calm.

We have a three man team on the boat. You always dive alone so there'll be two people up on top and one diving, and when that diver comes up then the next one goes in. Our fishing grounds range from the Mull of Kintyre in the south up to Cape Wrath in the north. We hug the coastline, because that's where the scallops are, but we will head over to the Western Isles in the summer, which is 52 miles away.

I know it's 52 miles because I rowed it last August. Five of us, all well into our fifties, we rowed from Stornoway back to Ullapool, it took us 14 hours 20 minutes. The weather was against us and three of the rowers had bad seasickness, so testament to them that they saw it through. And we raised over £30,000 for the MS Society. We got such a good welcome when we got back into Ullapool, I was gobsmacked, it was brilliant. We could barely walk when we got ashore, we were all just hanging on to each other.

Large starfish will take even mature scallops. We'll come across a scallop with a starfish wrapped around it, and the starfish pushes its stomach inside the scallop shell and devours it that way. Quite gross really. But generally, once scallops get somewhere that's suitable for them, if they're getting a good tide flow and good feeding and nothing's bothering them, I think they're pretty lazy really. They'll happily just sit where they are, getting fed.

Gary Lewis
Skipper of the *Donna Marie INS 17*

Scallops

The sound and smell of scallops sizzling in a pan with butter really is hard to beat, and with cracked black pepper and a sprinkling of salt they really are mouth-watering. We would always recommend cooking all of the scallop and have never understood why some people remove the orange roe—it is the reproductive organ, and for us it has a delicious and different taste and texture. Scallops can be bought dredged or hand-dived—we always get hand-dived ones as it's a much kinder way of treating the seabed and everything that lives there. If this is important to you and you would prefer hand-dived scallops, then always ask how your scallops where caught before buying.

There isn't a best time to eat scallops, but through summer they have better feeding so meat tends to be fuller. Scallops are hermaphrodites, meaning they have both male and female organs, and they produce both eggs and sperm to reproduce. The only time really to avoid them is when there's an algae bloom.

Scallops can be kept live in their shells for up to three days: keep them in a tub with a damp towel over them. To check that they're still alive, make sure the shells are tightly closed or, if they're open, that they close when you give them a good tap. You can keep shucked scallops for up to three days in the fridge and they freeze really well: we've tasted lots of fresh and frozen scallops, and if they're vacuum-packed and frozen on the day they were caught you really can't taste the difference.

How to Shuck a Scallop

You'll need a sharp but flexible knife
(something like a butter knife is good).

Place the scallop in your hand with the flat side facing upwards.
Insert the knife into the hinge end of the shell and twist to pop it
open. Wedge your thumb facing upwards inside the shell to keep
it open.

Slice the knife along the inside of the top shell, keeping it as
close to the shell as possible, to detach the meat. The shell
should pop a little bit open with your scallop meat still attached
to the curved side of the shell. Use your hands to open it up fully
and break off the flat top shell.

In the curved shell you will see the white meat and the orange
roe, the skirt, and the black stomach. Cut the meat in a straight
line along the hinge end of the scallop. Run the knife underneath
the roe and the white meat, cutting it as close to the shell as
possible. Try to do each incision in one swoop to prevent the
scallop meat from tearing. You'll be left with the white scallop
meat and the roe; discard everything else.

Give your scallops a quick rinse under cold water.

TIP: Don't take the roe off.
Lots of people do but it's
a real waste since there's
so much flavor in it and it's
delicious. The roe is also
packed full of essential
vitamins and nutrients so we
consider it to be a superfood!

  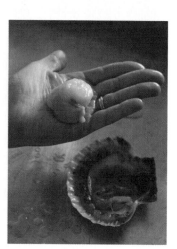

Cheesy Scallops

Honestly, if you love scallops and you love cheese this is a must-do recipe! It's also a great crowd pleaser so perfect if you've got pals over for dinner.

Serves 4

Ingredients
16 scallops, shucked (page 126)
glug of vegetable oil
a small handful of parsley, chopped
4 lemon wedges
salt and black pepper

for the cheese sauce:
3½ tbsp (50 g) butter
1 tbsp all-purpose flour
½ vegetable bouillon cube
1¼ cups (300 ml) whole milk
2 cups (200 g) grated cheese (we use a mix of Parmesan and Gruyère), plus extra for the top

8 curved scallop shells, cleaned

Make your cheese sauce first. Melt your butter in a pan over medium heat, then stir in your all-purpose flour and the crumbled bouillon cube. Cook this off for a few minutes, stirring constantly so the flour doesn't burn. Slowly pour in the milk, constantly whisking until you have a thick, smooth white sauce. There are no rules so add more or less milk depending on how thick you like your cheese sauce. Now stir in your cheese and keep on low heat until it has melted.

Turn on your broiler. Dry the scallops well on paper towels to stop them spitting when you add them to the pan. Put the frying pan over high heat and add the oil. When it's good and hot, put in the scallops. You want to hear them sizzle—if they don't, your oil isn't hot enough. Don't move them around in the pan, just let them fry for a minute and get a nice caramel color. Season, then flip them over, season again, and cook for a minute on the other side.

Now place two scallops in each shell and pour over some of the cheese sauce. Finish with some grated Parmesan, then put on a baking pan under the hot broiler until the cheese starts to brown and caramelize. Serve with some chopped parsley and a wedge of lemon.

Barbecued Scallops with Chili and Lime Butter

These are always a crowd pleaser! There's a bit of prep to do beforehand but they are so worth it and get an incredible smoky flavor off the barbecue. If you don't fancy chili and lime, try any of our other butters on page 227.

Serves 4

Ingredients

16 medium/large scallops, shucked (page 126)
14 tbsp (200 g) salted butter, softened
½ tbsp red chili pepper, chopped
1 garlic clove, grated
juice of ½ lime
pinch of smoked paprika
salt and black pepper

8 curved scallop shells

Heat your barbecue to a high heat (if you don't have a barbecue you can always use your broiler). Once you have shucked your scallops, dry them on paper towels or a clean tea towel, and put two scallops into each shell. The shells are going to act as the pan on the grill. Season with salt and pepper.

Beat the softened butter with the chili, garlic, lime juice, and smoked paprika in a bowl and season to taste. Divide it among the eight shells, placing it on top of the scallop meat.

Put the shells on the grill, close the lid, and cook for five minutes, until the butter has melted and the scallops are just cooked through. If you don't have a lid, just cover your scallops with aluminum foil or the top half of the scallop shell. So simple and so delicious!

Pan-Fried Scallops with Caramelized Red Onions and Wild Rice

Sweet scallops, sweet onions, and wild rice to mop it all up—need we say more?

Serves 4

Ingredients

16 medium/large scallops, shucked (page 126)
a good glug of canola oil
10½ tbsp (150 g) salted butter, sliced
1 lemon, quartered

for the rice:

3½ tbsp (50 g) salted butter
dash of canola or vegetable oil
3 garlic cloves, finely chopped
4 red onions, thinly sliced
1 heaped tbsp honey or brown sugar
2 tbsp balsamic vinegar
1 tbsp redcurrant jelly or smooth cranberry sauce
1 vegetable bouillon cube
1⅓ cups (250 g) mixed long-grain and wild rice
a small handful of parsley, chopped
salt and black pepper

First make your caramelized red onion rice. Melt your butter and oil in a frying pan over high heat, then lower the heat, and add your garlic and onions. Fry them for at least 20 minutes until they are soft and caramelized. Turn up the heat and add your honey, balsamic vinegar, redcurrant jelly, and the crumbled vegetable bouillon cube. Season with salt and pepper and cook for another 10 minutes or until your onions are nice and sticky.

Rinse your rice under cold running water until the water runs nearly clear, then cook in boiling water until tender, but so it still has some bite to it (check the package instructions because cooking times vary). Drain and stir into the onions, then add your parsley and season to taste.

Dry the scallops on paper towels or a clean tea towel. Put the frying pan over high heat and add the oil. When it's nice and hot, add your scallops—you should hear them sizzle as soon as they hit the oil. Don't move them around in the pan, you want them to sear and get a nice caramel color. Pan-fry the scallops for a minute and season with salt and pepper, then flip them over, season, and cook for a minute on the other side.

Add the butter, and when it starts to foam, baste the scallops for a further 30 seconds. Keep your temperature at medium-high heat to help them caramelize, but turn it down a bit if your butter looks like it's burning.

Serve your scallops up on a bed of wild rice and pour over the buttery juices. Serve with a wedge of lemon.

Pan-Fried Scallops with Herb Butter and Crispy Chorizo

The scallops we get from Gary are big and juicy and super sweet—they are always a hit at the Shack, and we are lucky enough to have them lots at home too. This is one of our favorite ways of cooking them—it's quite rich, so is great with a nice fresh salad and some lemon and herb couscous (page 211).

Serves 4

Ingredients

16 medium/large scallops, shucked (page 126)
a good glug of canola oil
2¾ oz (75 g) Spanish dry-cured chorizo, chopped into small chunks
14 tbsp (200 g) butter, sliced
3 or 4 chives, chopped
a few sprigs of curly parsley, chopped
a few sprigs of dill, chopped
salt and black pepper

Dry the scallops well on paper towels or a clean tea towel (this stops them spitting when added to the hot oil).

Put the oil in your frying pan over high heat, then when it's nice and hot add the scallops—they should sizzle as soon as you put them in. Don't move them around the pan, you want to sear them to get a nice caramel color. Fry them for a minute, season with salt and pepper, then flip them over, season, and cook for a minute on the other side.

Add the chorizo, butter, and herbs, and as the butter starts to foam, baste the scallops for a further 30 seconds. Keep your temperature at medium-high heat to help caramelize your scallops more, but turn it down a bit if your butter looks like it's burning. Serve immediately.

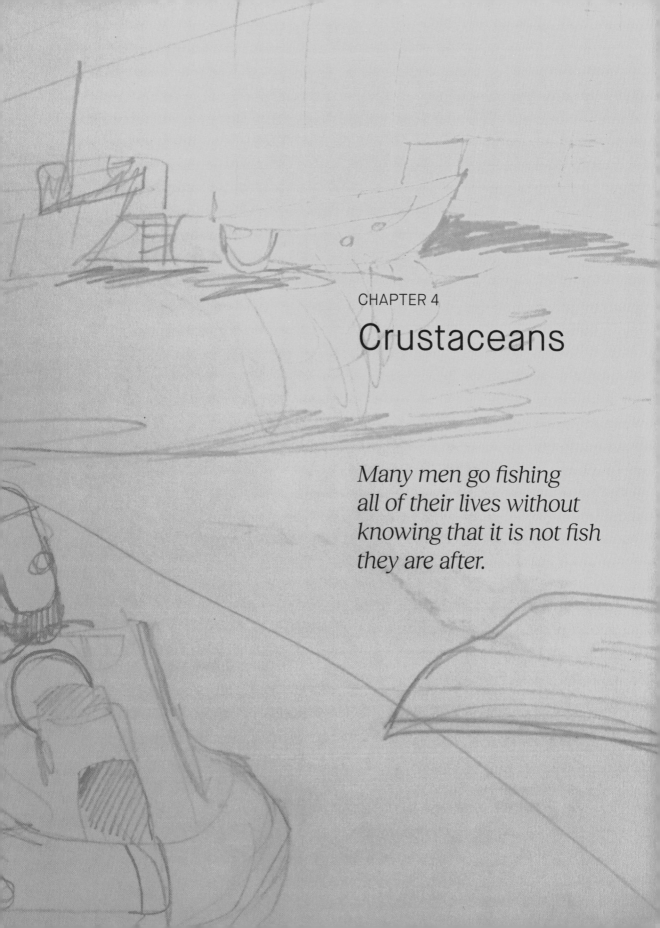

CHAPTER 4

Crustaceans

Many men go fishing
all of their lives without
knowing that it is not fish
they are after.

"I co-own a 10-meter creel boat fishing out of Ullapool. I started fishing at 23 and crewed on a few boats, then I bought my own boat at 25—just a small boat. I always had a love for the sea, for surfing and sailing, and I was always on boats but I never did any fishing when I was young. But where we're from it's all around you—there's friends at it, there's families at it—and I love it. I would have loved to get started earlier for sure.

The boat I own is a day boat, so we leave early in the morning, return in the evening. We're fishing crabs, langoustines, and lobsters—that's our main catch. We use creels or pots—a creel's just a trap on the seabed. It's got two eyes in it, which are just like doors and allow the shellfish to come in. They're attracted by the bait—every time we lift the creels we put in fresh bait. The shellfish smells this and they climb up through the eyes, into the creel. They can get in easily, but they can't get out easily. For langoustine, we're using salted herring as bait. We salt it, which brings out the oil so it's really smelly and the langoustine like that. For crabs and lobsters we're using fresh bait, stuff we've caught ourselves or frames from the fishmongers—the skeletons, the heads, the tails. There's not much wasted.

We like to get around our creels every two or three days, get the catch out, rebait, and get it back down. But crabs, lobsters, langoustine, they can all filter feed so if there's no predators about and they're not attacking each other, they can sit for a week quite happily in the pot. Our main predators are octopus, and they're very clever. They'll work their way along into the creel, they'll kill all the shellfish, then they'll get out and work their way along to the next one. So if your pots are down for a long time you can have a lot of damage by one or two octopus.

Lobsters live in shallower water in rocky, seaweedy areas. They like to hide in small caves, boulders, cracks, crevices, things like that. So if we're fishing for them we're usually fishing near the shores, round the islands. It's quite a skill— you're using your initiative to find them. Crabs, they're living out in the sand or in shells, in big, flatter areas. The crabs will move around a lot more than lobsters, so you follow them into deeper and shallower water, you're just following them around. Langoustines live in the mud in deep water, or shallower water in the summer. They burrow down into the mud, then come out to feed or to wander about and that's when we catch them.

We chose creel fishing just because it's a bit more sustainable. All the bycatch and most importantly all the small shellfish are returned to the sea completely unharmed, alive. It's dropped over the side and will go back down to the sea bed to live another day, to grow bigger. With trawling you're taking everything, so 90% of what comes aboard is dead or close to dead. If it goes back over the side, it's got next to no chance of survival. So creels are definitely a more friendly way of fishing.

The vast majority of our shellfish through the winter months goes to Keltic Seafare. He'll put it to hotels and restaurants around the Highlands, and what he can't sell here will go on the sleeper train down to the markets in London to be sold there. If there's big fishing and we're catching a lot of stuff, the extra will go to Europe. Through the summer months a good bit of our select or prime shellfish goes into The Seafood Shack.

There is good money to be made in fishing but people have to be prepared to pay for it. The boys are going out and it's a dangerous and a hard job. It takes a hunter-gatherer kind of skill to finding the things and making the boat pay. If you put all the hours into the money you get, you're probably working for minimum wage. You've got to love it and I feel very lucky that I do.

A lobster is one of only two animals in the whole world that in theory can live forever. If they're in perfect condition, with no predators and no disease, a lobster can just regenerate itself and keep growing and growing. If there's nothing to eat it and no disease it's going to catch, it can live forever."

Josh Talbot
Skipper of the *Bon Ami UL 77*

Lobsters

There are two opinions we always hear about lobsters: half think they are the most delicious seafood out there and just can't be beaten, and the other half think they are completely overrated and just not worth the money. Well, we're right in the middle! We don't get the people who can't see past lobster, but we also think there's something pretty special about them. Even the sheer look of them, so solid and hardy and fierce: you wouldn't want to mess with them. They really are the king of shellfish. They have beautiful colors: if you're lucky enough to come across a bright blue lobster, they really are the coolest looking creatures. Don't be scared of lobsters pinching you when you buy them alive; they should always come with their claws banded up and this will stop them from getting you.

Lobsters are most abundant here from June to October, since they tend to move to deep waters and feed less in the winter months. As the water temperature rises, the lobsters become more active, moving to shallower ground to feed, which makes them a lot easier to catch.

They aren't the easiest to cook since it doesn't take long to overcook them and that really does ruin a lobster. It's not easy to know what's going on in that shell when it's boiling away. We go for the general rule of better undercooked than overcooked; after all, when you split your lobster in half, the tastiest thing to do is finish it off in a pan over some butter, so you can perfect it then! When you cut a cooked female lobster in half you will often see the (unfertilized) red roe inside. If you have undercooked the lobster to pan-fry or grill later, the roe will still be black, which some people find a bit alarming! Don't worry, it's delicious and there's nothing wrong with eating it. When you finish cooking the lobster, as soon as the black roe has turned red, you'll know it's cooked to perfection.

We always cook our lobsters with the bands left on. It's not worth trying to get the bands off when they're alive since that may end in a nasty nip. Also, if you start pulling lobster claws around they can sometimes drop a claw as a defensive mechanism—something they'll do in the wild because they can regrow a new one. Often people think live lobsters are red when in fact they're blue. When you cook them they turn a deep red color and it's always a lovely transformation to watch.

We would keep a cooked lobster for up to two days in the fridge. The meat stays fresher out of the shell than in so if you know you're not going to eat them for a few days then it's a good idea to pick all the meat. You can always keep live lobsters in the fridge for up to two days—as long as they're not disturbed they'll just sit there—but you want to make sure the lobsters you buy are nice and strong and see all their legs and claws moving.

How to Cook Lobsters

We cook our lobsters for slightly less time than is often advised, then if we're having them cold (in salad, for instance) we just let them cool naturally as they will continue cooking after you remove them from the water. If the recipe requires cooking them some more—say, pan-fried or grilled lobster— we submerge them in cold water as soon as they're drained.

For 2 medium-sized lobsters (2-3 lb/1-1.5 kg each):

Fill a large pot three quarters full of water and add a couple of tablespoons of salt.

Bring the water to a rapid boil and add the live lobsters to the pot, making sure all the claws and legs are fully submerged. Have some tongs at the ready to push down the lobsters if needed. Medium lobsters will need to cook for eight minutes and will turn a deep red color once cooked.

Drain the lobsters and leave to cool.

TIP: Remember, cooking time will vary with the size and number of lobsters in the pot. So, adjust your time accordingly (e.g. four lobsters would take around 10 minutes).

TIP: There are so many different suggestions for how to initially kill lobsters before cooking; for example freezing them first, stabbing them between the eyes, etc. Personally, we find if you make sure your water is boiling like mad and you don't overfill the pan with lobsters, they will die extremely quickly and efficiently.

How To Dissect a Lobster

This is the fun but messy bit. Make sure you have some paper towels ready to wipe up; you'll need it!

You'll need: a chopping board, sharp knife, preferably not your best one, tea towel, rolling pin, pick

First place your chopping board on a flat surface. Place the lobster flat on the board and cut the bands off the claws. Break off the legs and set aside. Put your knife tip vertically on the cross of the head. Stretch out the tail of the lobster so it is flat, now press down with your knife, breaking the shell, and cut right through to the bottom of the lobster. Turn the lobster around 180° and repeat in the opposite direction through to the tip of the head, cutting the lobster in half. Pop to one side.

Using your hands, break the claws off the large legs. Grab your first claw and put it on the board. Using the sharp end of your knife throughout, hit the claw on its curved side about halfway down the shell to make an incision. Turn it over and repeat on the other side, then hit the middle of the claw to crack it (you may have to do this a couple of times). Once you have cracked both sides, the bottom part of the shell should come away. Hold onto the small pincher (the one that moves back and forth). Very gently pull the pincher out, hopefully taking the cartilage with it. Don't worry if it doesn't come out; you just need to remove all your claw meat, slice it in half, and remove the cartilage yourself.

Now get the two large legs that you removed the claws from. By hand or using a shellfish crusher, break them in half and use a pick to get the meat out of them. They are the sweetest and, we think, most delicious pieces.

If you're not satisfied you don't need to stop there—there's lots of yummy meat in the small legs. Place them on the board. Using a rolling pin, roll from the top to the bottom and (if you're lucky) the meat will slide out.

TIP: Be sure to keep all the shells—they can be used to make a delicious bisque.

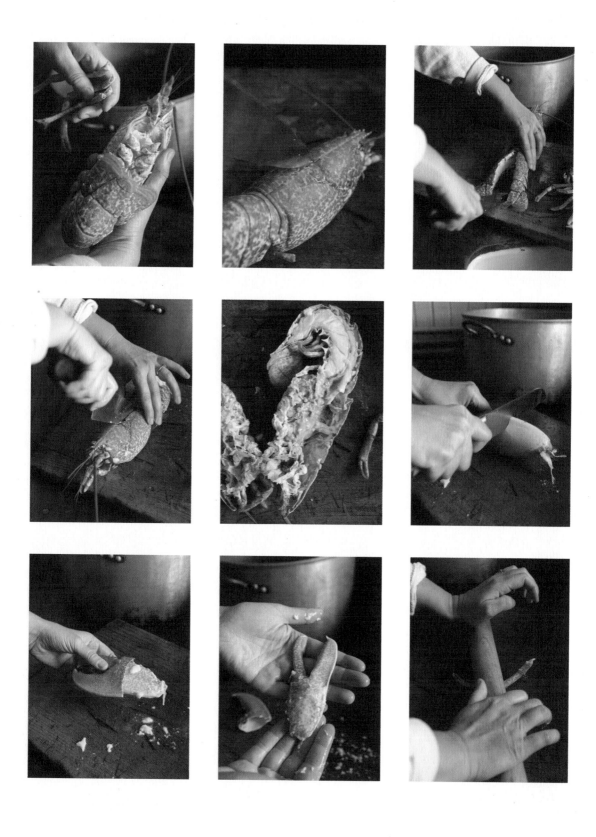

Lobster Bisque

Bisques can be time consuming to make, but man are they worth it: there's just something so satisfying about transforming a pan of rough and tough looking shells into a deliciously rich and smooth soup.

Serves 4

Ingredients

2 lobster shells, including legs
    and claws
2 bay leaves
7 tbsp (100 g) butter
glug of canola or vegetable oil
2 garlic cloves, chopped
2 red onions, chopped
2 white onions, chopped
2 red bell peppers, chopped
3 carrots, chopped
2 celery sticks, chopped
sprig of thyme
2 tbsp tomato paste
2 heaped tsp curry powder
1 heaped tsp smoked paprika
5 dashes Tabasco sauce
juice of ½ lemon
2 tbsp all-purpose flour
1 fish bouillon cube
½ vegetable bouillon cube
⅔ cup (150 ml) heavy cream
    (optional)
salt and black pepper

Always make sure to not overfill your pot with water when making your stock, since you can soon lose the flavors of the lobster. You can use any crustaceans you like—crab and langoustines work really well. To make enough bisque for four people you need 2 to 4 pounds (1 to 2 kilos) of shells. Always try and get bodies as well as claws, since they are to thank for most of the flavor.

First put your lobster shells in a large pot and cover with plenty of water—you want it to be at least a few inches above the shells. Throw in your bay leaves, bring to a boil, and then turn down to a very low simmer. Leave it to bubble away with a lid on for at least an hour—you're trying to extract all the flavor from the lobster shells so the longer you can leave it the better, just make sure to keep the lid on so your water doesn't evaporate. Once you're happy with your lobster stock, pour it through a colander into a bowl, then strain in a sieve to make sure you've removed every last little bit of shell.

While your stock is simmering put another large pot over medium heat and melt your butter and oil. Add in all your vegetables—garlic, red and white onions, red peppers, carrots, and celery—and the thyme, and sweat them down for about 20 minutes until they are soft and golden and have started to caramelize. Keep stirring so nothing sticks and, if you need to, add more butter. The longer you sweat your vegetables the sweeter they become—sometimes we sweat them for up to 45 minutes depending on how much time we have. Add your tomato paste, curry powder, paprika, Tabasco, lemon juice, and flour and crumble in the fish and vegetable bouillon cubes. Cook for another few minutes, stirring to stop anything sticking. Slowly pour in 6¼ cups (1.5 liters) of the lobster stock, and simmer for about fifteen minutes.

TIP: You'll have plenty of lobster stock left over so freeze it to use for future bisques. The soup itself freezes well too—freeze before you add the cream.

TIP: Lobster bisque can be a very rich soup, so if you'd like, add half a 14 oz (400 g) can of chopped tomatoes just before you blend everything together.

Blend everything up with a stick blender until the bisque is silky smooth. Bring back to a boil, then lower the temperature, add your cream if you're using it, and simmer very gently for a further five minutes. Taste your soup and season to your liking. We like to serve our lobster bisque with some fresh lobster pieces on top for some extra fanciness.

Pan-Fried Half Lobster with Parsley and Chive Butter

Once you have cooked the lobsters this is actually a pretty simple recipe, but don't underestimate it. Keeping it simple can be key to making something delicious.

Serves 4

Ingredients

2 cooked lobsters, submerged in
 cold water straight after cooking
 (page 143)
10½ tbsp (150 g) salted butter,
 chopped into chunks
a small handful of chives, chopped
a small handful of parsley,
 chopped
juice of ½ lemon
salt and black pepper

Halve your lobsters and break off the legs and claws. Crack the claws, but don't take the meat out of them. Place your butter and herbs in a large frying pan (don't use a nonstick one since the shells can scratch it and ruin the surface) and put it over high heat. Once your butter starts to foam, put in your lobsters, claws, and legs—if you don't have a big pan you may have to do this in two batches.

Fry your lobsters for around five minutes, constantly turning them in the herby butter as you go, then add the lemon juice and season with salt and pepper. Take off the heat and serve. Be extra careful you don't overcook your lobsters—they become rubbery very quickly.

TIP: You can tell when a lobster is overcooking if the meat of the body starts to curl out of the shell.

Lobster Burger

Served in a bun with ripe avocado and a dollop of fresh lemon mayonnaise, this is every bit as good as it sounds. We especially love how the breadcrumbs are so light they just add a little bit of crispiness to the lobster without overpowering it at all.

Serves 4

Ingredients
2 lobsters, cooked and halved
  (page 143)
1 egg, beaten
4 gourmet burger buns
1 tbsp vegetable or canola oil
4 tbsp lemon mayonnaise
  (page 225)
3½ oz (100 g) baby salad greens
  or gem lettuce
2 avocados, sliced
salt and black pepper

for the breadcrumbs:
3 slices white bread
small handful of fresh herbs
  (we use parsley and dill)
zest of 1 lemon

Set the lobster legs and claws aside, and carefully remove all your meat from the half shells. Slice the meat in half horizontally, leaving you with eight pieces. You can also add the claw meat if you want to have a bigger burger, but if not save it for another recipe.

Next, make your breadcrumbs: simply blend the white bread, chopped herbs, and lemon zest in a food processor until you have fine crumbs. Mix your lobster pieces with the beaten egg in a bowl and then add in your breadcrumbs, mixing everything around so the lobster gets nicely coated. Season well with salt and pepper.

Pop your burger buns in the toaster to get them crispy. Get a nonstick frying pan and heat up your oil so it gets real hot. Add your lobster pieces and fry them for only around 30 seconds, tossing halfway through. Don't overcook since the lobster can go rubbery very quickly. Once golden and heated through, drain on paper towels to remove any extra oil.

Now to assemble your lobster burger! We put lemon mayo on the bottom of the bun, then a handful of salad greens, followed by two pieces of lobster and a few slices of avocado. Season with salt and pepper and add a wee bit more mayo to top it off.

In the Shack we serve this with red cabbage slaw on the side (page 202).

TIP: It's the tender "melt in your mouth" piece of lobster that MAKES this burger so make sure you don't overcook it.

Barbecued Lobster

Put this on the menu and everyone will want to come to your barbecue! You can't beat the smoky sweet flavors you get from cooking lobster over charcoal, and it's super quick and easy. Keep an eye on it though, as you don't want the lobster to overcook. We serve this with a nice crispy salad and chunky bread.

Serves 4

Ingredients

2 cooked lobsters, submerged in
  cold water straight after cooking
  (page 143)
7 tbsp (100 g) salted butter,
  softened
a few sprigs of parsley, chopped
3 or 4 chives, chopped
a few sprigs of dill, chopped
juice of ½ lemon
salt and black pepper

Halve and dissect your cooked lobster as per the instructions on page 144. Get your barbecue good and hot.

In a bowl, beat the butter with the parsley, chives, dill, and lemon juice and season with salt and pepper. Add the meat from the lobster legs/claws to the half shell (we always put it into the head of the lobster), then divide the butter into four portions and smear it over your lobster halves, making sure it is spread over all the meat.

Put the lobsters on the grill shell side down, close the lid, and cook for five minutes or until the meat is piping hot. If you don't have a lid, cover the lobsters with aluminum foil before you grill them.

Lobster Macaroni and Cheese

This is the fanciest mac and cheese we've ever made; it brings together Scottish fine dining and home comfort and it really works. Another huge seller at the Shack!

Serves 4

Ingredients

1 medium-large cooked lobster
14 oz (400 g) macaroni
10½ tbsp (150 g) salted butter
2 white onions, thinly sliced
2 garlic cloves, finely chopped
½ small red chili pepper, sliced
1 vegetable bouillon cube
3 heaped tbsp all-purpose flour
approx. 2½ cups (600 ml) whole milk
12 oz (350 g) good quality Cheddar cheese, grated
handful of dill, chopped
handful of chives, chopped
salt and black pepper

TIP: Add some oil to the drained pasta to stop it sticking together. We never rinse our pasta after cooking as this removes the starch.

First, dissect your lobster as described on page 144, and take all of the meat out of the shell. You should have, in total, two body halves, your claw meat with the cartilage discarded, the meat from the legs, and any meat you can get from the small legs. Chop it all up into chunks and pop in a bowl in the fridge for later.

Now bring a large pot of water to a boil and add the macaroni. Cook for six or seven minutes—you want it to still have a little bite so always check the suggested cooking time on the package and take a couple of minutes off. Make sure you give it a stir from time to time so it doesn't stick to the bottom of your pot. Drain and return to the pot.

Get another pot and put it over medium heat to melt your butter. Once melted, add your onions, garlic, and chili and crumble in the bouillon cube, then lower the heat and sweat for at least 15 minutes until everything is very soft and golden and starting to caramelize. Keep stirring to make sure nothing burns. Once you are happy with your sweated onion mixture, add the all-purpose flour. Cook this off for another three minutes, stirring constantly so the flour doesn't burn. Slowly whisk in the milk, constantly mixing until you have a thick, smooth white sauce—there are no rules so add more or less milk depending on how thick you like your cheese sauce. Now add your cheese and stir over low heat until it has melted, which won't take long. Add the drained macaroni, the lobster meat, and the dill and mix so everything is well covered with the sauce. Season to taste and serve on its own with a sprinkling of chopped chives on top. Amazing.

Crab

Crab has to be the most undervalued shellfish. It's delicious, but the mess and fuss of cooking it must put people off, which is actually pretty understandable. We buy brown Atlantic crab, caught out in our Scottish seas, but you can use your favorite local variety. There are two types of meat in a brown Atlantic crab. There's the white meat, which is flaky and delicate in flavor, and you want to be gentle with it since it's easily overpowered. Then there's the brown meat, which is the total opposite and has a mushy texture and a strong flavor; some people love it and some loathe it! It's worth finding out which side you're on.

You can mix the two together which is a great combination, or you can use them separately—it's up to you. When you're cooking live crab, their claws can be a bit scary, but don't worry—the tendons in the claws are always nipped by the fishermen. This stops the crabs being able to close their claws so they don't kill each other in the tanks on the boats. You can test this out by putting something in the middle of the claw to see if it closes—maybe don't use your finger though, just in case.

Fresh crab can be kept in the fridge for three days in the shells and no longer than four days if the meat has been picked. You can also keep crab alive in the fridge for up to three days —just pop a damp cloth over them in the bottom of the fridge.

You can buy crab all year round but they are in their best condition in the winter months after feeding all summer. There is a big difference between the meat in the female and male crabs. Female crabs have smaller claws so therefore less white meat, but the bodies can be full of brown meat. The males have much larger claws—so plenty of white meat—but don't have any brown meat in the bodies. So, depending on your preferred meat, it's always worth checking if you're buying a male or female crab.

How to Cook Crab

To cook 4 medium-sized brown Atlantic crab
(approx. 1 lb 12 oz/800 g each):

Fill your biggest pot three-quarters full of water and add two
tablespoons of salt. Bring the water to a rapid boil and put
in the live crab, making sure all the claws and legs are fully
submerged. If you don't have a pot big enough for all, then
cook them in two batches. Depending on the size of the crabs,
boil them for eight to 10 minutes if you have two in the pan,
and 12 to 14 minutes if you have four. Drain and cool under cold
running water.

How to Dissect Crab

Twist off all the legs, small and large. Sometimes the feathery grey gills called "dead man's fingers" will come out with the large claws—these are not good to eat and will make you feel sick so make sure to discard them. Most of the time they will be in the body.

Put the crab on its back so its tummy is upwards. You will see the crab's two eyes, and below these there are two small flaps. Move these aside and push down on the slightly softer shell underneath with both your thumbs. Push hard to crack through, then you can pull out the middle section of the body. Inside it looks like a bit of a mess, but you can eat everything EXCEPT the "dead man's fingers." Don't worry, they are so distinctive you can't miss them—they look just like feathers. Pick through the rest of the meat and put it in a bowl. This is where you will find most of the brown meat.

Now have a wee tidy up and start removing the white meat from the leg and claws. Get the larger legs first and tear the claw from the leg. There will be two small pieces of cartilage—just make sure they don't go into your crab meat bowl. Use a pick or a claw tip to get the meat from the leg.

Now for the claw. Get a large, heavy spoon or a knife (choose one you're not that fond of). Place the claw flat on a board and crack it in the middle with the blunt side of your knife or the curved side of the spoon, then turn it over and do on the other side. You may need to do this a few times; it gets easier with practice! Remove the bottom part of the shell and you should be left with half a cracked claw. Give it a rinse to remove any loose shell. You can either leave them like this or get all the meat out with a pick—just watch out for the large thin piece of cartilage in the middle.

Always make sure you thoroughly pick through your white crab meat since you'll often find small pieces of shell in it. There's nothing worse that chewing down onto a hard piece of shell!

Crab and Sweet Corn Soup

Crab meat and corn is a classic combo for good reason, and in this tasty broth it adds a bit of sweetness to the crab stock base. We like to eat big bowls of it with crusty warm bread. Cook the stock for as long as you can to extract every last bit of flavor from the crab shells.

Serves 4

Ingredients

6 cooked crab claws, dissected and picked (keep your shells), page 157–158
3 bay leaves
10½ tbsp (150 g) salted butter or mixed herb butter (page 227)
dash of vegetable or canola oil
3 onions, thinly sliced
2 garlic cloves, finely chopped
½ red chili pepper, thinly sliced
2 celery sticks, thinly sliced
2 medium carrots, peeled and thinly sliced
1 x 11 oz (325 g) can of corn, drained
a few dashes of Tabasco sauce
4 tbsp all-purpose flour
1 fish bouillon cube
1 vegetable bouillon cube
small handful of parsley, chopped
juice of ½ lemon
salt and black pepper

Put your white crab meat into a bowl, and your crab claw shells in a large pot with the bay leaves. Fill the pot with water—you want double the amount of water as crab claws, if not more. Put a lid on and bring to a boil, then lower the heat to a very gentle simmer and cook for at least an hour to get all the flavor out of the crab shells.

Melt your butter and oil in a large pot over high heat and add your onions, garlic, chili, celery, carrots, and corn. Turn the heat down to medium and sweat the veg for at least 20 minutes, until everything is really soft and sweet. Stir in the Tabasco, flour, and the crumbled bouillon cubes and cook off for another five minutes, stirring all the time. Once done remove from the heat.

Once your crab stock is ready, pour it through a colander into a pot or bowl, then strain through a sieve to make sure there are no tiny bits of shell. Put your vegetables back on the heat and, once hot, slowly whisk in 6¼ cups (1.5 liters) of the crab stock, stirring all the time. Take your time—it can go lumpy if you add the stock too fast. Once all your stock is added, bring to a boil and cook for a further 10 minutes, and then turn down to a low simmer and add your crab meat, parsley, and lemon juice. Taste and season with salt and pepper if it needs it—it may be salty enough. Serve steaming hot.

Crab Bisque

This soup takes a bit of time and effort but it's worth it! Use a mix of body, leg, and claw shells to make the bisque, just be sure to remove the "dead man's fingers."

Serves 4

Ingredients

dash of vegetable or canola oil

7 tbsp (100 g) salted butter

2 garlic cloves, chopped

1 white onion, chopped

1 red onion, chopped

2 celery stalks, chopped

1 large carrot, chopped

2 red bell peppers, chopped

1 vegetable bouillon cube

2 tsp smoked paprika

2 tbsp tomato paste

2 bay leaves

juice of ½ lemon

a few dashes of Tabasco sauce

scant 1 cup (200 g) canned
  chopped tomatoes

approx. 2¼ lb (1 kg) crab shells

2 heaped tbsp cornstarch

⅔ cup (150 ml) heavy cream

salt and black pepper

Put a large pot over medium heat, and add your oil, butter, garlic, white and red onions, celery, carrot, and red peppers. Sweat for around 20 minutes, stirring every now and then, until your veg is all delicious and caramelized. Now stir in your crumbled vegetable bouillon cube, smoked paprika, tomato paste, bay leaves, lemon juice, and Tabasco and fry it all for a further five minutes. Add the canned tomatoes and the crab shells. Give it a good mix and then cover with boiling water: you want about double the amount of water to shells and veggies, no more. Bring to a boil, pop a lid on it, and cook at a gentle simmer for at least an hour. The longer you cook your bisque, the more flavor you will get.

Once you're happy with your bisque, strain it into another pot through a sieve, discarding the shells and veggies. Do this twice to remove any trace of shell. Put the bisque back on the heat and bring back to a boil. In a cup, mix your cornstarch with a tablespoon of water and add it to the pot, then simmer uncovered for another 15 minutes. Add as much or as little cream as you want and season to taste. Serve with some warm crusty bread.

TIP: If you want to add a little more pizzazz to this already delicious bisque, then serve with some fresh white crab meat and grated parmesan on top.

Hot Garlic Crab Claws

This falls apart in your mouth, almost like a (much quicker) seafood version of slow cooked lamb. Crab claw meat is so delicate in flavor that for this recipe we don't think it needs any spices or herbs in the melted butter apart from garlic. Yum!

Serves 4

Ingredients

7 tbsp (100 g) salted butter

2 garlic cloves, skin left on and
crushed with the back of a knife

12–16 cooked crab claws,
cracked but not picked
(page 157)

salt and black pepper

Put your butter and the squashed garlic cloves in a pan over high heat and give it a good stir as it melts. When the butter starts to foam, add your crab claws. Lower the heat to medium and season with salt and pepper. Keep turning your claws in the butter so it gets into all the meat but watch out it doesn't start to burn. After about five minutes, put a lid on and leave it on really low heat for five to 10 minutes, making sure you turn the claws every now and then to ensure they don't burn, and to spread that yummy garlic butter all over. By cooking them slowly and over low heat, the crab claw meat becomes super soft and melt-in-your-mouth delicious. Serve with some bread and salad.

Potted Crab

This is a real crowd pleaser and can be made in advance so it's all hit and no hassle. We usually use white crab meat, but if you've got some brown you can use a mixture. Make sure you serve it with warm toast so the butter topping melts!

Serves 4

Ingredients

10½ oz (300 g) cooked white
  crab meat
3 tbsp mayonnaise
½ red chili pepper, deseeded and
  finely chopped
small handful of chives, chopped
juice and zest of 1 lime
salt and black pepper

for the butter topping:
14 tbsp (200 g) butter
2 tsp paprika

Pick through your crab meat to make sure there are no little bits of shell and put it in a bowl. Mix in the mayonnaise, chili, chives, and lime juice and zest. Taste and season if it needs it. Divide among four ramekins and flatten the top using the back of your spoon so it's nice and even.

Melt the butter in a pan and add the paprika. Pour a thin layer over the crab and put the ramekins in the fridge to cool. Serve with warm crusty toast and a wedge of lime on the side.

Variation: Potted Langoustine

We make a langoustine version that's just as good. Just slice up 16 cooked langoustines (or use jumbo shrimp) and mix with three tablespoons crème frâiche, a handful of chopped dill, and a half teaspoon of cayenne pepper. Add the juice and zest of half a lemon and season with salt and pepper. Top the ramekins with melted roasted garlic and chive butter (page 227) and set in the fridge. Serve with toasted bread and a handful of arugula leaves on top.

TIP: This will keep in the fridge for up to four days.

Hot Dressed Crab

This recipe was a tester that Kirsty came up with, and it just worked from the first time she made it. It's been on our menu ever since and is a great way to use both the white and brown meat.

Serves 4

Ingredients

4 cooked crabs, dissected and
  white meat picked (page 157–158)
3½ tbsp (50 g) butter
2 scallions, finely chopped
2 garlic cloves, finely chopped
1 small red chili pepper, finely
  chopped
1 tbsp sweet chili sauce
1 tsp finely minced ginger
1 tsp paprika
small handful of parsley, chopped
2 slices of white bread, processed
  into breadcrumbs
1 lime, quartered
salt and black pepper

Preheat your oven to 425°F (220°C) or turn on your broiler. Remove the brown meat from inside the crabs and place in a bowl with the white crab meat from the claws. Remember to discard the "dead man's fingers." Give your crab body shells a good wash.

Pop your butter in a small frying pan over high heat, and once it's sizzling add the scallions, garlic, chili pepper, sweet chili sauce, ginger, and paprika. Sweat down for a few minutes and then put in your parsley and the crab meat and stir until hot. Season to taste. Pop it all back in the crab shells, top with your breadcrumbs, and then place in the oven or under the broiler and cook until the breadcrumbs go crispy and brown. We serve these with some good quality toasted bread, a wedge of lime, and a big, fresh arugula salad.

Crab, Mango, and Avocado Salad

These ingredients make such a perfect combination: the saltiness of the crab, the sweetness of the mango, and the earthy flavors of the avocado mixed together with fresh lime and crunchy snap peas—OK, we could go on and on. It creates a perfect summer salad.

Serves 4

Ingredients

7 oz (200 g) mixed salad greens (we like to use arugula, watercress, and baby leaf salad)

10½ oz (300 g) white crab meat or 6 cooked crab claws, dissected and picked (page 157–158)

1 mango, cut into small chunks

1 avocado, sliced

2 scallions, thinly sliced

handful of thinly sliced cucumber

handful of cherry tomatoes, quartered

handful of snap peas, thinly sliced

small handful of parsley, roughly chopped

Parmesan, grated (optional)

salt and black pepper

for the dressing:

1 tbsp sweet chili sauce

1 tbsp olive oil

juice and zest of 1 lime

This is so easy. First make your dressing by whisking the sweet chili sauce, olive oil, and lime juice and zest in a cup. Pop your salad greens in a large salad bowl and add the crab meat, mango, avocado, scallions, cucumber, tomatoes, snap peas, and parsley. Pour over the dressing and toss lightly but thoroughly, then taste for seasoning and add salt and pepper if needed. If you like, top with some grated Parmesan.

TIP: If you want a bit of spice, add some finely chopped red chili pepper.

Crab and Avocado Rolls

These rolls are simple and delicious and they never last long when we've got them on the menu. They're great for picnics or for taking to work.

Serves 4

Ingredients

9 oz (250 g) crab meat (or meat
  from about 5 cooked crab claws)
½ red chili pepper, finely chopped
2 scallions, finely chopped
juice and zest of ½ a lime
2 avocados, sliced
small handful of parsley, chopped
1 tbsp crème frâiche
1 tbsp mayonnaise
4 bread rolls
butter, for spreading
handful of salad greens for
  each roll
salt and black pepper

In a bowl, mix your crab meat, chili, scallions, lime juice and zest, avocado, parsley, crème frâiche, and mayonnaise and season to taste. Cut the rolls in half—if you like you can toast them—and butter both sides, then pile the crab filling onto the bottom halves. Add some fresh salad greens to each one and put the roll tops back on.

Variation: Langoustine and Avocado Rolls

We sometimes make a langoustine version which is just as tasty. Mix 32 cooked and peeled langoustines (or use jumbo shrimp) with 4 tablespoons of Marie Rose sauce (page 225) and season to taste. Butter 4 rolls and fill each one with a sliced half avocado, then the langoustines, then a handful of salad greens.

Creamy Crab Linguine

This is a lovely way to turn crab into a main meal. You can use white crab meat on its own, or if you prefer a richer flavor use a mixture of white and brown. Either way it's delicious. If you've got any of our chili, paprika, and lime butter (page 227), use it to fry the shallots—we always do!

Serves 4

Ingredients

splash of vegetable or canola oil
3½ tbsp (50 g) butter or chili, paprika, and lime butter (page 227)
4 shallots, sliced
6 scallions, thinly sliced
2 garlic cloves, chopped
½ red chili pepper, chopped
1 vegetable bouillon cube
½ fish bouillon cube (optional)
a good glug of white wine
1 heaped tbsp crème fraîche
⅔ cup (150 ml) heavy cream
1 lime, zested and then halved
10½ oz (300 g) white crab meat (or a mixture of white and brown)
small handful of parsley, chopped
14 oz (400 g) linguine
3½ oz (100 g) Parmesan, grated
4 handfuls of arugula
salt and black pepper

Heat a frying pan over medium heat and add a splash of oil and the butter. Let the butter melt and then stir in the shallots, scallions, garlic, and chili. Sweat them for around 10 minutes until the onions are soft; the longer you cook them the tastier your finished dish will be! Crumble in your bouillon cubes and cook until they dissolve into the onions.

Add the white wine, crème fraîche, cream, and lime zest, then throw in the lime halves and simmer over medium heat for around five minutes. Stir in the crab meat and parsley.

In a separate pot, boil the linguine for six to seven minutes—you don't want to overcook it since it will keep cooking when you add it to the sauce. Give your pasta a stir hallway through to make sure it isn't sticking together. When it is cooked, drain in a colander, leaving a small amount of cooking water in with the pasta so it doesn't get sticky. Don't rinse the pasta, since you want to keep the starch to thicken the sauce.

Reduce the heat under the sauce and gently toss in the pasta, making sure each strand of linguine is coated in sauce and crab. Taste to check for seasoning and add a dash more cream if you want.

Once dished up, sprinkle freshly grated Parmesan on top and add a handful of fresh arugula. Serve with a wedge of lime.

Crab Cakes

Everybody seems to love a crab cake! We only use white crab meat in ours, but if you have some brown meat then mix that in too for a richer flavor. Serve them up with sweet chili mayo (page 225), green salad, and lemon and herb couscous (page 211) for a dinner that will go down well with all the family.

Serves 4

Ingredients

14 oz (400 g) white crab meat
 (or mix of white and brown)
14 oz (400 g) potatoes, peeled and
 chopped into large chunks
1 fish or vegetable bouillon cube
3 scallions, sliced
2 garlic cloves, finely chopped
½ red chili pepper, thinly sliced
small handful of parsley, chopped
small handful of dill, chopped
small handful of chives, chopped
juice and zest of 1 lime
scant ½ cup (50 g) all-purpose
 flour
2 eggs, beaten
salt and black pepper

for the breadcrumbs:

4 slices white bread
small handful of parsley
small handful of chives
zest of 1 lime
salt and black pepper

vegetable oil, for frying

TIP: To freeze, wrap the uncooked crab cakes individually in plastic wrap and defrost fully before frying.

Pick through your crab meat for any bits of shell, making sure you do this thoroughly since it's easy to miss out tiny wee pieces that can be detrimental to somebody's tooth! Put your potatoes into a pot and cover with cold water. Add two pinches of salt, bring to a boil, and then simmer until soft. Once they slide off a knife inserted into the middle, drain and let them steam-dry—this bit is important since you don't want the crab cakes to be too wet. Put your bouillon cube in a small mug and cover it with a tablespoon or so of boiling water. Mix it until it dissolves into a runny paste. Add this to your potatoes and mash them. Once you've gotten rid of all the lumps, stir in your crab meat, scallions, garlic, chili, parsley, dill, chives, and the lime juice and zest. Mix it all together until completely combined, taste, season, and add more of any flavor if you think it needs it. Divide into eight equal portions and roll each one into a ball between your palms to make eight crab cakes.

To make your breadcrumbs, process the bread, parsley, chives, and lime zest in a food processor until you have fine crumbs. Place your flour in one bowl, beaten eggs in another, and breadcrumbs in a third and season each bowl. Dip each crab cake into the flour, then the eggs, and then the breadcrumbs, making sure they are fully coated at each stage. Now to cook your crab cakes: we deep fry ours, but you can pan-fry them if you prefer. If you're deep frying, slowly heat enough vegetable oil to fully submerge a crab cake to 350°F (180°C) in a deep fryer or large pan. Put your crab cakes in the hot oil (do a couple at a time) and cook for about five minutes, until the breadcrumbs are golden and crispy and the crab cake starts to float. Being careful since your oil will be very hot, remove them with a slotted metal spoon and drain on paper towels. If you are pan-frying them, heat a small amount of vegetable oil and fry your crab cakes for around five minutes on each side, until golden and crispy.

Langoustines and Spineys

Langoustines, also known as Scottish prawns, are delicious little beasties. The smaller ones are sweeter, but you get much more meat out of the claws in larger langoustines. Spineys, or squat lobsters, are similar to langoustines but a bit smaller and more squashed looking. They are delicious and even sweeter than the langoustines.

Langoustines can be trawled or caught by creels. There are arguments for and against either method, but we feel creel fishing is more sustainable, so we choose to buy creel-caught rather than trawled. Creel-caught langoustines are more expensive, but you always get them alive and they tend to be bigger and a higher quality. We think they're worth it. You can buy them all year round, but we avoid May as this is when they tend to cast their shells which can make them soft and tasteless. If you can't find them in your region, you can buy frozen langoustines online, or substitute jumbo shrimp.

You can't go wrong when cooking langoustines, they don't take long to cook, and you can always pull one out mid-cooking and crack it open to check how it's doing. The cooked shells will turn a deeper pink and the meat will turn from translucent to white. Spineys are much smaller than langoustines—we always tail them before cooking since there's no worthwhile meat in the bodies or claws. Because they are so small, they only take a matter of seconds to cook and we always plunge them in cold water immediately afterwards to ensure they don't carry on cooking as they cool.

You can eat langoustines and spineys cold but we would always choose to have them hot, which makes them much softer so they really melt in your mouth.

We would only keep cooked langoustines in the fridge for up to two days; it's just not worth keeping them any longer since they lose their sweetness and start to taste a bit fishy—that's when you know it's time to bin 'em! You can keep langoustines alive for one day in the fridge before you cook them but not for any longer as they start to kill each other.

Spineys are totally different and only have a shelf life of a day before they start to turn black. This is why there's no market for them and they're such a local treat, so if you want to buy them make sure they're on the menu that night; it's a bit sad if you've saved them for lunch the next day and then wake up to find they've gone a very unappealing black color.

How to Cook Langoustines

Back in the day, fishermen would cook their shellfish in sea water. They would say the saltier the water, the sweeter it makes the shellfish, and it definitely works! So don't panic if you ever put too much salt in your water; it won't ruin your shellfish.

Fill a large saucepan three-quarters full of water and add a good handful of salt—a couple of tablespoons is about right. Bring the water to a rapid boil, then add the live langoustines to the pot—making sure they are all submerged—and cover with a lid.

Medium langoustines will need to cook for four minutes—they will turn a deeper shade of pink as they cook. To check they are done, take one out using some tongs and break its tail away from its head. The insides should be white and opaque, not translucent. Drain in a colander and let the langoustines cool.

How to Peel Your Langoustines

Most people just use the meat from the tails of langoustines, but if you have time we really recommend removing the meat from the claws also. It is time consuming but always worth it.

To start, twist the tail of the langoustine away from the head, and pull off the two large claws. Discard the head or keep it to make langoustine stock if you like—just use our lobster bisque recipe (page 146) and replace the lobster shells with langoustines.

To remove the tail meat, hold the shell in the middle and break along the joint that runs from left to right—you will feel a small crack either side. Be gentle as you don't want to rip it completely in half. Now pull off the small end of shell, leaving the tail half in the shell and half out. Now wiggle the rest of the meat gently out of the shell and you should end up with a full tail.

Now to extract the meat from the claws: break them at the joint and use a claw or a pick to get the meat out of the small leg. To get the meat from the claw, gently pull out the pincher (the piece that you can move back and forth) and you should get some meat on the cartilage that comes with this. Now carefully crack the top of the claw open, using a cracker or by pressing down with a knife onto a chopping board (we use our teeth), and pick out the meat inside.

 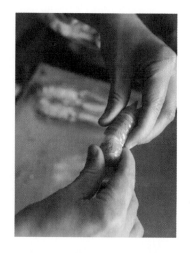 

Butterflied Chili Langoustine Bagel

We like to do this on a hot, summery day, since bagels and salad just feel like a summer brunch. If you don't like or don't have bagels, just use a burger bun. If you can't find langoustines, you can substitute jumbo shrimp.

Serves 4

Ingredients

20 langoustines (about 2¼ lb/
  1 kg), cooked and peeled
  (page 179)
4 tbsp crème frâiche
juice and zest of 1 lime
4 bagels, halved and toasted
guacamole (page 201)
glug of vegetable or canola oil
4 handfuls of baby salad greens
2 scallions, finely sliced
salt and black pepper

for the breadcrumbs:
3 slices white bread
2 garlic cloves, roughly chopped
½ red chili pepper, roughly
  chopped
1 tsp smoked paprika
small handful of parsley,
  finely chopped

Butterfly your langoustines by cutting from top to bottom of each one, making sure you don't cut all the way through. Then make your breadcrumbs: pop your bread, garlic, chili pepper, smoked paprika, and parsley in a food processor and process to crumbs. Place in a bowl and season with salt and pepper, then mix in your langoustines—they are usually a bit wet so the crumbs will stick without needing any eggs.

Mix your crème frâiche with your lime juice and zest and season with salt and pepper. Spread each of your bagels with the creme frâiche on one half and guacamole on the other. Now put your oil in a frying pan or wok over high heat. Once hot, add your langoustines and toss around for a minute or so until the breadcrumbs are golden and crispy. Drain on some paper towels and place five langoustines on top of the guacamole in each bagel. Top with a handful of salad greens and scallions and then finish off with your crème frâiche-spread bagel. So good!

Pan-Fried Langoustines with Garlic and Thyme Butter

Josh cooked these langoustines for Mary Berry on the beach with some (a lot) of guidance from her. She told the cameras it was the most delicious thing she'd ever eaten, so naturally Josh still brags about it!

Serves 4

Ingredients
10½ tbsp (150 g) salted butter
4 garlic cloves, skin left on and
  crushed with the back of a knife
4 sprigs of thyme
32 langoustines (about 4 lb/1.7 kg),
  cooked (page 179), or substitute
  shell-on jumbo shrimp
salt and black pepper

Place your frying pan over high heat and add your butter, whole garlic cloves, and thyme. Cook until the butter melts and your thyme start to sizzle.

Pop your langoustines in the pan and season with salt and pepper (you may need to do this in a couple of batches, depending on the size of your frying pan). Turn the heat down to medium and every now and then toss the langoustines about to make sure they are cooking evenly and aren't burning on the bottom. If the pan gets a bit dry add more butter, since the langoustine shells tend to soak it up. If you have a lid, pop that on to help keep all the flavor in. You don't want to overcook the langoustines, just heat them all the way through and let them soak up the garlicky butter.

Once they are nice and hot, serve them with some warm crusty bread and a wedge of lemon.

Variation: With Chili, Garlic, and Lime
Omit the thyme and add a red chili pepper, halved lengthwise, a teaspoon of smoked paprika, and a couple of halved limes squeezed into the pan at the same time as the garlic.

Moroccan-Style Langoustine Rice

This is a great dish for a dinner party—it's not too difficult to make and is almost a one-pot wonder. If you feel like you want something on the side, serve it with a big fresh salad. If you can't find langoustines, you can substitute jumbo shrimp.

Serves 4

Ingredients

24 langoustines (about 3 lb/
    1.3 kg), cooked (page 179)
1 bay leaf
juice of ½ lemon
3½ tbsp (50 g) butter
glug of vegetable or canola oil
1 white onion, finely chopped
2 garlic cloves, finely chopped
½ red chili pepper, thinly sliced
½ in (1 cm) piece fresh ginger,
    peeled and grated
3 scallions, trimmed
    and chopped
1 x 14 oz (400 g) can chickpeas,
    drained and rinsed
handful of green beans,
    ends trimmed
1 tsp ground cumin
1 tsp ground coriander
2 tsp paprika
1 tsp turmeric
1 cup (200 g) basmati rice
4 tbsp crème fraîche
salt and black pepper

TIP: If you don't have time to make langoustine stock for your rice, don't worry. Just cook it as instructed on the package and save your shells for another day.

Peel your langoustines (see page 180) and pop the shells in a large pot and the meat in the fridge for later. Cover the shells with at least twice as much water, and add your bay leaf, lemon juice, and a good grind of pepper. Bring to a boil, turn the heat down, and simmer with a lid on for at least 30 minutes to make a stock for your rice to cook in later.

Place your frying pan over high heat and add the butter and oil. Once it's melted, turn the heat down to medium and add your onion, garlic, chili, ginger, and half of your scallions. Sweat for about 10 minutes over low heat, making sure nothing burns. Stir in your chickpeas, green beans, cumin, coriander, paprika, and turmeric and cook for another five minutes, then remove from the heat.

Rinse your rice in cold water until the water runs clear. Strain your langoustine stock through a fine sieve into a big bowl and pour about 4¼ cups (1 liter) into a pot. Pop it back on the heat and bring to a boil, then add the rice and simmer for eight minutes—you want your rice to still have a bite to it. Drain it through a sieve.

Place your chickpea and onion mixture back on the heat and stir in your reserved langoustine meat and the drained rice. Cook, stirring gently, until everything is piping hot. If it looks too dry, add a splash more stock to loosen it to a good consistency. Season with salt and pepper and sprinkle with the remaining scallions, then serve with a dollop of crème fraîche.

Super Green Thai-Style Langoustine Curry

When you're feeling like you need a good boost of green veggies in your life, this recipe is the business. Go crazy if you want and even throw in some snap peas; you can't overdo it with the greens!

Ingredients

glug of vegetable or canola oil
1 white onion, finely chopped
½ red onion, roughly chopped
1 small green chili, sliced
3 garlic cloves, finely chopped
½ in (1 cm) piece fresh ginger, thinly sliced
1 vegetable bouillon cube
2 heaped tbsp Thai green curry paste
1 heaped tsp honey
2 x 14 oz (400 ml) cans coconut milk
2 tbsp soy sauce
a few good splashes fish sauce
1 tbsp sweet chili sauce
10½ oz (300 g) jasmine rice
24–30 langoustines (about 3 lb/ 1.3 kg), cooked and peeled (page 179), or substitute jumbo shrimp
5¼ oz (150 g) broccoli, sliced
2 limes, halved
4 big handfuls curly kale, roughly sliced
1 zucchini, very thinly sliced
4 scallions, thinly sliced

TIP: The curry base freezes really well—freeze before you add in the langoustines and vegetables since they're always so much better fresh.

First, heat up your vegetable oil in a frying pan over medium heat. Add your white and red onions, chili, garlic, and ginger and fry for around 10 minutes, until really soft and golden. Then turn the heat up a bit and add your vegetable bouillon cube, green curry paste, and honey. Fry for another five minutes.

Keeping the heat at medium, add your coconut milk, soy sauce, fish sauce, and sweet chili sauce. Simmer for 10 minutes or so until the sauce has thickened up and smells lovely and fragrant.

While it simmers, put a pot of water on to boil and cook your rice for eight minutes so it still has a little bite. Drain.

Gently stir your langoustines and broccoli into the coconut sauce and squeeze in your lime halves. When the curry comes back up to a boil, add your kale and the rice and cook for a few minutes, stirring, until the kale is tender. Quickly stir in the zucchini slices and serve topped with the sliced scallions.

How to Cook Spineys

Spineys, also known as squat lobsters, are hard to find. They are caught on the west coast of Scotland and if you are lucky enough to find some, buy them. They are truly delicious—we think they're even better than langoustines. There's no market for them since they don't keep well and go black quickly, so they are a true local delicacy. Cook them and eat them on the same day for a real treat. You need about 40 spineys for four people.

Because spineys have next to no meat in their claws and bodies, we always tail ours before cooking. Ask your fishermen for tailed spineys, but if you get them whole it's simple to do yourself. Just pull the head and claws to one side and give it a wee twist to break apart from the tail. Fill your pan three quarters full of water and add a good handful of salt. Bring the water to a rapid boil, then drop in the spiney tails, making sure they are all submerged, and cover with a lid. Cook for no longer than a minute, then drain them in a colander and submerge into cold water—spineys are small so can overcook very quickly. Drain again and toss in lemon juice before putting in the fridge. Eat the same day.

How to Peel Spineys

The easiest way to peel spineys is to stretch the tails open with the shell facing down. Use your thumb to push the meat from the bottom of the tail (i.e. the end that wasn't attached to the body) so it slides out the other end. The meat should poke out the top and you just need to pull it out. Much easier than cracking open the shell each time!

Spiney Popcorn

Everyone should try these! Sweet spineys in a light and crispy tempura batter are the perfect snack, especially dunked in roasted garlic mayonnaise. They cook in moments and are a hot favorite with locals at the Shack. You can substitute langostines or shrimp.

Serves 4

Ingredients

10½ oz (300 g) spineys
    (or shrimp), cooked and peeled
    (page 190)
scant 1 cup (110 g) all-purpose
    flour
1 lemon, quartered
roasted garlic mayonnaise
    (page 225)
salt and black pepper

for the tempura batter:

1¼ cups (150 g) all-purpose flour
¾ cup (100 g) cornstarch
2 tsp baking powder

vegetable oil, for deep frying

To make your batter, put the all-purpose flour, cornstarch, and baking powder into a bowl. Using an electric mixer or whisk, slowly add approximately 1¼ cups (300 ml) water, mixing all the time, until your batter is a thick but runny consistency. It should stick to your finger when you dip it in and there should be no lumps. Season the batter well with salt and pepper.

Carefully heat the vegetable oil to 350°F (180°C) in a large pot or deep fryer. Coat your spineys in the flour, then dip them into the batter—because they are so small this can get a bit messy. Place them in the hot oil, being super careful not to burn your fingers. You'll probably need to fry them in batches depending on the size of your pot. Give your oil a stir with a metal spoon to make sure the spineys don't stick together and fry them for no longer than a minute; if they don't crisp up in that time then your oil isn't hot enough.

Drain on some paper towels and serve immediately with some salt and pepper, a wedge of lemon, and the roasted garlic mayonnaise on the side.

"I started lobster pots when I was still in school. I had maybe a dozen or so that I used to row out to the mouth of the loch. I started off rowing and then I graduated to a bigger boat with an outboard motor. Then I was a year in Strathclyde University so there wasn't any lobster fishing done then. When I packed it in and came back to Ullapool I was getting odd berths on different fishing boats, one of them being a boat from Skye which my father ended up buying. So then we made 200 prawn creels and we made everything, the frames, the lot. We started fishing in the spring of '68 with that boat. Then my father and I bought the *Harvest Lily* between us, 50 years ago as of Easter past.

We had to tail all our prawns [shrimp] back then; there was no market for the whole fish. That changed in, I think, '72. I remember the first time we started landing whole prawns in the *Harvest*, John Britten was my crewman and Murdo the Pope, as we called him. John knew about the no-more-tailing business but Murdo didn't, and John said, 'Oh, I'm not going to bother tailing them.' Murdo said, 'You have to!!' 'No, I'm not doing it!' That was the first time we made £100 for a day with the creels. All in for £5 per stone which is 6.3 kg or something. There was no grading, no small, medium or large; it was just all thrown in a box.

We mostly just fished all round Loch Broom itself, and I worked a lot beyond Black Isle and the pockets of ground out there. We used to rotate the creels around the grounds and they always got a rest, which doesn't happen now. There was space to do that then. We had 200 creels and we would haul them three times per day and sometimes you'd get as much after four hours as you'd get overnight, like a full fish box out of 50 pots.

I bought the *Albion* in the back end of 1973 and went trawling with that. To begin with we were catching spurdog—it used to be sold in the chip shops in England as rock salmon. That was the first money I made trawling. I'd never been at the job before. When we went prawn trawling later on in the springtime we would make as much in two days as the creel boats were making in a week. Half our catch was fish as well as prawns. There were no quotas of any description then, of course, so we could land more or less everything we caught apart from undersize fish. The prawns were crazy large when you think about it now.

I consider the creeling now to be a rat race. At least with the trawl everybody gets the same fair chance at the ground because people move around—when the fishing goes off, you move somewhere else. You can't really do that with the creels because there's nowhere left to go. The ground is jammed up with creeling gear because it stays there all year. I used to take my gear ashore maybe in September when the mackerel fishing was heavier going in the Minch—there was quite a danger of losing your gear with the mackerel boats. I never had to clean it: it would clean itself when it was lying ashore in the rain and snow, and it wasn't in the water long enough to get so dirty either, so it was nice and fresh when it went back out again after New Year. In the late 70s up to '87 it was possible to catch half a ton of live prawns in a day with less than a thousand pots. You'd be lucky to do that in a week now. Creels are hard on the ground when they're on it 365 days a year—it's not getting a chance to recover.

There's less and less trawlers to be honest. Boats used to be based in Lochinver and Gairloch and Mallaig and places like that, and now they've all been cut up and the guys that I knew are long gone.

It's patchy, but it's always been patchy. Way back, when there was too much small fish in the ground you wouldn't catch prawns in the trawl because they wouldn't come out of the burrows, then when the small fish disappeared you'd get the prawns. See, monkfish and cod are nibbling away at them as well. When they first started trawling for prawns in the Minch in the '50s, 60 or 70 years ago, eight stone of tails for a three- or four-hour tow was considered quite a good haul. They were all quite big prawns but they weren't big actual numbers. Now you'll get hauls of 30 stone, lots of actual numbers but smaller prawns. It's something of a strange one.

My son Ruaridh started going to sea with Murdo Urquhart in the summer holidays. He's been mad for it ever since he got a dinghy and a few creels. I think he's the fifth generation of us that's fished. My mother wasn't very happy when I jacked in university and went to it, but it's just what I always wanted to do, messing about in boats. Fishing lobster is the most interesting job in the world, it's the only job I would ever have done if I could have made a living at it. Somehow there are more lobster on the go now than there seemed to be when I was trying to catch them.

My father would salt his own herring for eating. He salted tons of it for bait which you never even had to buy back in the day; we used to shovel it off the pier. All we had to buy was the salt. Anyway, he used to salt his own herring for eating and he would then lift them out of the little salt barrel, put them in a bucket of fresh water overnight, maybe two or three times to get the salt away, and then you'd have them with nice potatoes with the skins falling off, usually home-grown as well. I used to like the roe out of them. I could really go a bundle on that."

Roy MacGregor
Skipper of the *Harvest Lily*, the *Albion*,
Headway UL 3 and *Sustain UL 45*

CHAPTER 5

Sides

Only dead fish swim with the stream.

Guacamole

Mmmmm guacamole!! We could both eat avocados every day. It goes without saying you must make sure your avos are SUPER ripe before using—it makes all the difference.

Serves 4

Ingredients
2 very ripe avocados, halved and pitted
1 garlic clove, crushed then finely chopped
¼ red onion, finely chopped
½ small red chili pepper, finely chopped
handful of cherry tomatoes, chopped small
juice of ½ lime
pinch of ground cumin
salt and black pepper

Scoop out all your avocado into a bowl and mash with your fork until it is almost smooth—we like to leave it a bit chunky. Add all of your other ingredients to the bowl and stir until everything is mixed in, then season to taste.

Tomato and Cilantro Salsa

This is such a lovely light and tangy salsa, and it gives a super fresh taste to any pan-fried fish.

Serves 4

Ingredients
6 super ripe tomatoes (or 30 cherry
  tomatoes), chopped
½ small red onion, finely chopped
1 garlic clove, crushed then finely chopped
½ red chili pepper, finely chopped
small handful of fresh cilantro, finely chopped
juice of ½ lime
½ tsp sugar
salt and pepper

Mix everything together and season to taste.

TIP: If you can, make this a few hours before you want to eat it, since the flavors enhance over time.

Red Cabbage and Carrot Slaw

This is a really popular side dish at the Shack. The crème frâiche makes it nice and light, perfect to go with burgers or smoked fish.

Serves 4

Ingredients

1 medium red cabbage, thinly sliced
1 small carrot, peeled and grated
1 red onion, thinly sliced
3 heaped tbsp mayonnaise
2 heaped tbsp crème frâiche
1 tsp sugar
a good splash of white wine vinegar
handful of dried cranberries (optional)
salt and black pepper

Add all your ingredients together, give it a good mix, and then season to taste.

TIP: If we're doing a big batch, we always use a food processor for the veggies, using the slicing disc for the cabbage and the shredding disc for the carrot.

Quinoa, Cabbage, and Sweet Corn Salad

Quinoa works really well in any salad because it keeps a bit of bite when it's cooked. This one's packed full of color and makes you feel good just looking at it.

Serves 4

Ingredients

½ cup (100 g) quinoa
½ vegetable bouillon cube
1 x 11 oz (325 g) can of corn, drained
1 tsp smoked paprika
½ cup (150 g) frozen petits pois (petite green peas)
4 large handfuls of mixed salad greens
 (we use chard, spinach, and arugula)
7 oz (200 g) red cabbage, sliced paper thin
4 scallions, thinly sliced
seeds from 1 pomegranate

for the dressing:
4 tbsp olive oil
4 tbsp honey
4 tbsp cider vinegar
salt and pepper

About an hour before you want to eat, put your quinoa in a saucepan and cover with water so it's around a thumbnail higher than the grains, then crumble in the bouillon cube. Bring to a boil, cover, and then simmer for about 20 minutes. You will know it's ready when the quinoa looks like it's popped open—if it looks like it's drying out before it's properly cooked, add a bit more water. As soon as it's ready, put it in a bowl and put it in the fridge.

Preheat your oven to 425°F (220°C). Put your corn in a single layer on a baking pan, sprinkle with the smoked paprika, and season with salt. Roast for around 30 minutes, until the kernels start to crisp and go brown—watch the kernels around the edges since they seem to catch pretty quickly and burn. Boil your peas until they are just cooked and still bright green, then refresh under cold water, drain, and add to the quinoa in the fridge to cool. Put your salad greens, cabbage, and scallions in a large salad bowl. Once your quinoa and peas have cooled, toss them into the salad with the roasted corn and the pomegranate seeds. (You can add the corn either warm or cold; it's great either way.)

To make the dressing, shake your olive oil, honey, and cider vinegar in a wee jar with some salt and pepper, and then pour over the salad. Give it all a good toss and serve up.

Roasted Beet, Feta, and Mint Salad

This is so easy and can be bulked up by adding some arugula and watercress. It is a lovely side for pan-fried smoked mackerel (page 92) and crispy potatoes, and it is also perfect for summery barbecues!

Serves 4

Ingredients

10½ oz (300 g) raw beets, peeled and cut into ¾–1 in (2–3 cm) chunks
glug of olive oil
1 tbsp honey
1 tbsp balsamic vinegar
3½ oz (100 g) feta, crumbled
juice and zest of 1 lime
handful of fresh mint, chopped
salt and black pepper

Preheat your oven to 350°F (180°C). Pop your beets on a baking pan, season with salt and pepper, and coat with a glug of olive oil and the honey and balsamic vinegar. Roast for 20 minutes until just tender.

Put the beets in a bowl and add your feta and the lime juice and zest. You can either have this warm or wait until your beets have cooled down before you add your feta and lime. Serve topped with the chopped fresh mint.

Sweet Roasted Root Vegetables

This is a great recipe to do when you've got a fridge full of vegetables that need using up. You can substitute the veg for anything you want, just make sure to adjust your cooking times—for example, if you're using broccoli, put it in near the end since it cooks a lot quicker than carrots. Sometimes we add a handful of toasted sliced almonds at the end for a bit of extra crunch.

Serves 4

Ingredients

2 raw beets, peeled
1 butternut squash, skin left on, seeds discarded
1 red pepper, deseeded
2 red onions
1 carrot, scrubbed
2 garlic cloves, skin left on and crushed
good glug of olive oil
2 tbsp balsamic vinegar
2 tbsp honey
4 handfuls of baby spinach
3½ oz (100 g) feta, crumbled
handful of toasted sliced almonds (optional)
salt and black pepper

Preheat the oven to 400°F (200°C). Cut your beets, squash, red pepper, red, and carrot into roughly the same sized chunks so they cook in the same time. Put them all on a large baking pan in a single layer and toss with the garlic and a good glug of olive oil. Season well.

Roast in the oven for 20-30 minutes until the veg is just starting to soften but still has a good crunch. Take out of the oven and drizzle with the balsamic vinegar and honey, tossing to make sure all the vegetables are well coated. Then turn up the heat to 425°F (220°C) and pop the pan back in for another 15 minutes until everything is tender and caramelized but not soggy. Take your vegetables out, mix in the spinach and feta, sprinkle with the almonds (if using), and serve immediately.

Wilted Nutmeg Spinach

A side that goes with pretty much any white fish and takes minutes to make.

Serves 4

Ingredients

3½ tbsp (50 g) butter

½ tsp nutmeg, freshly grated

10½ oz (300 g) fresh spinach

salt and black pepper

Heat your butter over medium heat, then add your grated nutmeg, and fry for a minute. Chuck in the fresh spinach and turn every 10 seconds or so—it will only take a minute to wilt. Season with salt and pepper and serve straight away.

TIP: Don't overcook the spinach—it will literally take a minute to wilt, and it goes watery and slimy if you overdo it.

Caramelized Red Onion Wild Rice

This is one of our favorite side dishes. It goes perfectly with scallops but is just great with almost anything!

Serves 4

Ingredients

3½ tbsp (50 g) butter
glug of vegetable or canola oil
3 garlic cloves, peeled and finely
 chopped
4 red onions, thinly sliced
1 tbsp honey or brown sugar
2 tbsp balsamic vinegar
1 vegetable bouillon cube
1⅓ cups (250 g) mixed long-grain
 and wild rice
a few sprigs of fresh parsley, finely
 chopped
salt and black pepper

First melt your butter with a glug of olive oil in a frying pan over high heat. Add your garlic and onions, then lower the heat and slowly fry—you want them to caramelize so take your time and keep stirring and watching the heat so they don't burn. It will take at least 20 minutes. Increase the heat a little and add your honey, balsamic vinegar, crumbled vegetable bouillon cube, and salt and pepper, and cook for another 10 minutes or until everything is nice and dark and sticky

While your onions are frying, put a saucepan filled with water on to boil for your rice. Rinse the rice until the water runs nearly clear, then add it to the boiling water. Lower the heat to a simmer and cook until tender, but still with some bite, stirring only once (check the package instructions because cooking times vary). Test a grain, then drain the rice thoroughly—you don't need to rinse it. Add to the onions along with the parsley, toss it all together, and season to taste with salt and pepper.

TIP: Save some of the caramelized onions to make caramelized red onion butter. Just mix two tablespoons of the fried onions with 2¼ sticks (250 g) softened butter and roll up in some plastic wrap to store in the fridge or freezer. Perfect with any fish, meat, or veg!

Simple Lemon and Herb Couscous

We never follow the instructions on the back of the couscous package! They use way too much water and it always ends up mushy. At the Shack we use just enough boiled water to cover the couscous, which makes it much lighter and fluffier.

Serves 4

Ingredients

3½ tbsp (50 g) butter
1 vegetable bouillon cube
juice and zest of ½ lemon
1½ cups (350 ml) boiling water
1½ cups (250 g) couscous
handful of mixed fresh herbs, chopped (we use dill, parsley, and chives)
salt and black pepper

Put your butter, crumbled bouillon cube, lemon juice, and zest in a bowl and add the boiling water. Mix until the butter and bouillon have dissolved. Pour in your couscous—you want to make sure that it comes to no more than ⅛ inch (½ cm) below the water line. If you have too much water add more couscous and vice versa. Give everything a good mix, then cover and leave to stand for five minutes. Add your chopped herbs and some black pepper and mix again with a metal spoon, or if it's sticking together use a fork to fluff it apart. Taste and season with salt.

Variation: Beet Couscous

Just add a raw beet, peeled and grated, at the same time as the couscous.

Dauphinoise Potatoes

Creamy, cheesy, and garlicky potatoes—what more do you want? This is the dirtiest dauphinoise recipe we know.

Serves 4

Ingredients

2¼ lb (1 kg) white potatoes
  (or you can use a mixture of
  sweet potatoes and white)
pat of butter
2 white onions, sliced
3 garlic cloves, chopped
1 vegetable bouillon cube,
  crumbled
sprinkle of nutmeg
1¼–2 cups (300–480 ml) heavy
  cream
3½ oz (100 g) Parmesan, grated
salt and black pepper

Preheat the oven to 350°F (180°C). Peel and slice your potatoes very thinly and dry them with a clean tea towel or paper towels. Melt your butter in a sauté pan and add your onions and garlic, then sweat for 10 to 15 minutes until they are soft. Crumble in your bouillon cube and the nutmeg and season with salt and pepper, then fry for another five minutes. Stir in the potatoes and pour over enough cream to just cover, then season with salt and pepper. Bring up to just before a boil—you don't want your cream to boil or it will curdle—then lower the heat and simmer until the potatoes are just tender.

Pour everything into an ovenproof dish (we use the same pan that we cooked the potatoes in to save washing up but make sure it's ovenproof). Give it a shake so the potatoes are reasonably level on top, sprinkle over the Parmesan, and pop in the oven. Cook for around 20 minutes or until the parmesan is crispy and golden. Right at the end, you can turn the heat up to 425°F (220°C) to brown the top.

TIP: You can use ground nutmeg but you get so much more flavor by grating a whole one (and they keep forever).

Two Ways with Hot Potatoes

Crispy Herb Potatoes

Yummmm—crispy potatoes! These are a great alternative to fries and can be jazzed up with any herbs you have in the fridge. In the Shack we serve them with pan-fried smoked mackerel (page 92), but they're a great side to most fish and meat dishes.

Serves 4

Ingredients
1 lb 2 oz (500 g) baby potatoes
good glug of olive oil
3½ tbsp (50 g) salted butter
small handful of fresh parsley, finely chopped
small handful of fresh dill, finely chopped
salt and black pepper

Place your potatoes in a pot and cover with cold water, add a good sprinkle of salt, put the lid on the pot, and cook over high heat until a potato just slides off your knife when inserted into the middle. Drain the potatoes in a colander and let them steam-dry. When they are cool enough to handle, halve or quarter them.

Put your frying pan over high heat and add a good glug of olive oil. Get the oil nice and hot. Cook the potatoes in the oil for 10 minutes to get them really crispy—start with high heat and reduce if they start to burn. Keep stirring them so they don't stick to the pan, then after 10 minutes add the butter and keep cooking and stirring until you are happy with the crispiness. Remember: the crispier the better! Sprinkle in the herbs, season with salt and pepper, and serve.

Crushed Baby Potatoes with Butter and Herbs

This is a really easy way to transform your everyday baby potatoes into a lovely side dish. They are very popular at the Shack!

Serves 4

Ingredients
1 lb 2 oz (500 g) baby potatoes
3½ tbsp (50 g) salted butter
small handful of fresh herbs, finely chopped
  (we use parsley and dill)
juice of ½ lemon
salt and black pepper

Cook and steam-dry your baby potatoes, then put them back into the empty pot. Over medium heat, add your butter, herbs, and lemon juice and season well. Keep mixing your potatoes as the butter melts, slightly crushing them as you go to let all that yummy butter and herby deliciousness into them. Serve hot.

TIP: These can be kept in the fridge for three days. Why not throw them in the oven to reheat them and crisp them up?

Kale and Nutmeg Mashed Potatoes

This is a great way to turn mashed tatties into something posh and completely delicious!

Serves 4

3 lb 5 oz (1.5 kg) white potatoes
7 tbsp (100 g) salted butter
1 leek, sliced
4 handfuls of kale
1 tsp freshly grated (or ground) nutmeg
2 eggs
scant ½ cup (100 ml) whole milk
salt and black pepper

Peel and halve your potatoes, place them in a saucepan, cover with cold water, and add a couple of pinches of salt. Place over high heat, bring to a boil, and simmer until cooked. While your potatoes are cooking, put a frying pan over high heat and melt your butter. Turn the heat down to low and add your leeks, frying them until they're soft. Throw in your kale and the nutmeg and cook until the kale is just tender, then remove from the heat (you don't want your kale to go soggy).

Once your potatoes are cooked, drain and steam-dry for a minute, then return to the pan, add your eggs and milk, and mash until there are no lumps. Stir in your leeks and kale, season well, and serve.

Two Potato Salads

Shack Potato Salad

At the Shack we get a lot of compliments on this potato salad. Like anything simple, it's all in the details, so make sure your potatoes are perfectly cooked and you get that balance of sharp vinegar to sweet mayo right. It's particularly delicious if you serve it slightly warm.

Ingredients

1 lb 2 oz (500 g) baby potatoes
1 bunch scallions, thinly sliced
1 x 11 oz (325 g) can of corn, drained
3 heaped tbsp mayonnaise
1 tbsp white wine vinegar
salt and black pepper

Place your potatoes in a large saucepan and cover with cold water, then add a good sprinkle of salt and boil until a potato just slides off your knife when inserted into the middle. Drain and let them steam-dry in the colander. Once the potatoes are cool enough to handle, chop them in half or quarters depending on their size and place in a bowl.

Add the scallions, corn, mayonnaise, and white wine vinegar, then mix and season with salt and pepper to taste.

Lemon, Dill, and Crème Frâiche Baby Potatoes

This potato salad is at its best served straightaway when it's still a bit warm.

Serves 4

Ingredients

1 lb 2 oz (500 g) baby potatoes
3 tbsp crème frâiche
juice and zest of ½ lemon
a few sprigs of fresh dill, chopped
salt and black pepper

Cook and steam dry your potatoes as above. In a bowl, whisk your crème frâiche, lemon juice and zest, and dill together. Toss with your still-warm potatoes and eat immediately.

CHAPTER 6

Sauces & Dressings

There's two things a fisherman needs - a good engine and a good wife.

Quick and Easy Hollandaise Sauce

We got this foolproof hollandaise recipe from Kirsty Williams, a great family friend. It's now one of our go-to sauces at the Shack and never (touch wood) seems to curdle. It's worth using really good, organic, free-range eggs.

Serves 4

Ingredients
2¼ sticks (250 g) salted butter
3 large egg yolks
juice of ½ lemon
salt and black pepper

Melt your butter in a small pan over medium-low heat (or in a microwave). Take it off the heat as soon as it melts and pour into a jug. Pop your egg yolks in a small bowl, then using an electric mixer or whisk (which is better since your bowl will move around less) keep mixing as you very slowly drip in your butter. Keep it slow as this is when it can curdle. Once you've added half of your butter, you can speed up to a steady, slow pour. Mix in your lemon juice and season with salt and pepper. Done.

Homemade Mayonnaise

If you have time to make this, it's really worthwhile. It's not difficult and it tastes so different from the jar stuff!

Ingredients

2 egg yolks

1 tbsp white wine vinegar

1 tsp sugar

¼ tsp Dijon mustard

scant 1 cup (225 ml) sunflower or
   olive oil (or a mixture)

salt

Pop your egg yolks, white wine vinegar, sugar, and mustard in a bowl. Pour your oil into a measuring cup or pouring jug. With one hand, whisk the egg mixture with a whisk while slowly dripping your oil in with the other hand. Keep whisking as you drip in the oil and you will soon notice your mayonnaise thickening. Continue adding the oil in a steady but slow stream, always whisking—you can pour faster as it thickens up but be careful since the mayonnaise can curdle. Keep going until you've added all of the oil to the mayonnaise (which should take about five minutes) and season with salt to taste.

TIP: If your mayonnaise does curdle then don't panic—you can rectify it. Either beat in another egg yolk or get a clean bowl and put in two tablespoons of boiling water, then slowly whisk in your curdled mayonnaise until it smooths out.

Roasted Garlic Aioli

When we make aioli we always roast the garlic—it gets sweet and caramelized and is a winner every time.

Ingredients

1 whole garlic bulb

1 tbsp olive oil

2¼ cups (500 g) mayonnaise

a few chives, chopped

salt and black pepper

Preheat the oven to 250°F (120°C). Slice the bottom off the garlic bulb so the ends of the cloves are exposed. Now get a sheet of aluminum foil, scrunch it to make a small bowl, and put in your olive oil and a good amount of salt and pepper. Put your garlic bulb on top of the oil, cut side down. Wrap your foil over the top of the bulb to seal it in a parcel and cook in the oven for 45 minutes to an hour.

Check if it's ready by removing it from the oven and giving it a wee squeeze—it should be super soft. If it's not, put it back in the oven for another 10 minutes or so and cook until soft, but make sure you don't burn the bottom of the garlic.

Remove the garlic from the foil parcel, and once it's cool enough to touch, flake off any loose peel and squeeze the soft garlic cloves out of the skin. They should slide out easily. Place the roasted garlic flesh in a bowl and add the olive oil from the foil parcel. Mash it up with a spoon until it's smooth—pick out any stubborn hard bits. Add your mayonnaise and as many chives as you like, mix together, and season with salt and pepper to taste.

TIP: This always tastes better the day after since it gets even more garlicky overnight.

Tartare Sauce

Tartare sauce is just a great accompaniment for any fried fish. We put it in our fish finger sandwich (page 45) and it's delicious used in place of lemon mayo and pesto in our haddock wrap (page 42).

Ingredients
scant 1 cup (200 g) mayonnaise
2 small pickles
1 shallot, chopped
2 tbsp capers
½ tsp English mustard
1 tsp horseradish sauce
squeeze of lemon juice
pepper

Put all of your ingredients in a food processor and process until it's the consistency you like (we like it a bit chunky). Taste and add extra of anything you like to suit your taste buds.

Marie Rose Sauce

Marie Rose sauce always seems, well, a bit "old school" but it's still around for a reason. Mix it up with some fresh langoustines and a light salad—yum!

Ingredients
1¾ cups (400 g) mayonnaise
⅓ cup (100 g) ketchup
small squeeze of tomato paste
4 or 5 drops Tabasco sauce
1 tsp brandy (optional)
juice of ½ lemon
1 scant tbsp paprika
salt and black pepper

Mix everything together and season to taste.

Lemon Mayonnaise

A simple, go-to favorite with seafood.

Ingredients
1¾ cups (400 g) mayonnaise
juice and zest of 1 lemon
salt and black pepper

Mix everything together and season to taste.

Curried Mayonnaise

This is a great sauce to keep in the fridge, ready to use. The longer you leave it, the better it gets as the flavors infuse.

Ingredients
1¾ cups (400 g) mayonnaise
2 tsp curry powder
1 tsp smoked paprika
pinch of cayenne pepper
juice of ½ lemon
salt and black pepper

Mix all of your ingredients together and season to taste.

Mustard and Dill Mayonnaise

Dill and mustard are quite strong flavors but combined with sweet mayonnaise they make a lovely sharp dip, perfect to go with some battered oysters.

Ingredients
1¾ cups (400 g) mayonnaise
2 tsp Dijon mustard
a few sprigs of fresh dill, finely chopped
salt and black pepper

Mix all of your ingredients together and season to taste.

Shack Butters

These butters are really quick and easy and are a handy thing to have around to jazz up your seafood—in the Shack we use them instead of plain butter in most of our recipes. You can store them in the fridge for weeks or pop them in the freezer to take out when needed. All our recipes are made with 2¼ sticks (9 oz/250 g) of salted butter.

Method for all the butters:

Leave your butter out in a warm room for a few hours to soften or heat it in a microwave until soft. You don't want your butter to melt—you should just be able to make an indent with your finger.

In a bowl, mix all your chosen flavorings into the butter with a wooden spoon. We always season our butters with just a little amount of salt and some freshly cracked black pepper.

Get some plastic wrap and cut it so it is about 12 by 16 in (30 by 40 cm). Lie this out flat on your worktop and spoon the butter mixture across the middle in a horizontal line, leaving about a hand space on either side. Now hold the corners of the plastic wrap closest to you and fold them over the butter, running your hands along the butter to the edges to smooth it out and remove any air holes. Twist the plastic wrap at either end and gently roll your butter to form a good cylinder shape. Perfect for storing in the fridge and freezer!

Roasted Garlic and Chive

2¼ sticks (250 g) salted butter

1 roasted garlic bulb (page 223)

small handful of chives, chopped

Chili, Paprika, and Lime

2¼ sticks (250 g) salted butter

1 small chili pepper, finely chopped

½ tsp smoked paprika

juice and zest of ½ lime

Mixed Herb

2¼ sticks (250 g) salted butter

a few sprigs of parsley, chopped

4 or 5 chives, chopped

a few sprigs of dill, chopped

Lemon, Caper, and Dill

2¼ sticks (250 g) salted butter

juice and zest of ½ lemon

1 tbsp capers, coarsely chopped

a few sprigs of dill, chopped

Pesto

2¼ sticks (250 g) salted butter

1 heaped tbsp basil pesto or roasted red
  pepper pesto (page 229)

Saffron and Sweet Shallot

2¼ sticks (250 g) salted butter

1 shallot, finely diced

1 garlic clove, finely chopped

pinch of saffron

Put a teaspoon of the butter and your shallot and garlic in a small pan and sweat on low heat for 15 minutes or so until caramelized, turning the heat down if it looks like it's going to burn. Then proceed as above.

Basil Pesto

Pesto is just lovely, simple and fresh, and we use it all the time. In Ullapool in the spring we pick wild garlic that grows down by the river and add that in—if you can get hold of some, it's a massive bonus.

Ingredients
⅓ cup (50 g) pine nuts
3½ oz (100 g) fresh basil
2 garlic cloves, peeled
1¾ oz (50 g) Parmesan, grated
juice of ½ lemon
olive oil
salt and black pepper

First dry-toast your pine nuts in a frying pan over medium heat for about four minutes, until they go a golden brown and smell delicious. Pull the stalks off your basil and discard them, since they will make your pesto taste too strong. Pop the leaves into a blender with the roasted pine nuts, garlic, Parmesan, and lemon juice and blend. Then, with the blender still running, pour in the olive oil until you have a smooth paste that isn't too runny or too thick. Taste and season with salt and pepper if it needs it.

Variation: Roasted Red Pepper Pesto
Roast or grill three red peppers drizzled with a little olive oil until the skin starts to brown (about 30 minutes). Then add to the blender along with the ingredients above, reducing the quantity of basil to 1¾ oz (50 g).

TIP: It's worth doing a big batch of pesto as it will keep for months in the fridge. Put it in a jam jar and seal with a splash of olive oil. You can use it to whip up some pesto butter (page 227) to pop in the fridge or freezer.

Salad Dressing

We make all the dressings we use in the Shack. The important thing to remember is to use three parts olive oil to one part vinegar. Your dressing will easily last a month in the fridge—in fact they tend to taste better after a few days—so always make in big batches. You can alter the quantities as much as you want, just remember the 3:1 ratio and you can't go wrong!

For all the dressings (apart from the basil recipe), the basic method is the same:

Put your ingredients in a jam jar or dressing bottle. Give it a really good shake, taste, and add extra of anything to get the balance of flavors you like—sweet, salty, or punchy.

Honey Mustard Dressing

We use this dressing a lot in the Shack and have been asked for the recipe many times, so here it is!

Ingredients

1½ cups (360 ml) extra virgin olive oil
½ cup (120 ml) white wine vinegar
1 tsp wholegrain mustard
2 tsp runny honey
2 garlic cloves, crushed
salt and black pepper

Balsamic Dressing

This is a sweet and strong dressing. It can be overpowering so use sparingly.

Ingredients

1½ cups (360 ml) extra virgin olive oil
½ cup (120 ml) balsamic vinegar
1 tsp wholegrain mustard
2 heaped tsp dark brown sugar
2 garlic cloves, crushed
salt and black pepper

Anchovy and Caper Dressing

This dressing goes great with smoked fish, and we often use it to accompany smoked trout.

Ingredients

1 cup (240 ml) extra virgin olive oil
¼ cup (60 ml) lemon juice
1 garlic clove, crushed
a few sprigs of parsley, finely chopped
1 tbsp capers, rinsed and finely chopped
4 anchovy fillets, finely chopped
pepper

Chili Thai-Style Dressing

This dressing is great with the Thai-style cod fishcakes (page 56). We tend to make it to use fresh (though it does keep fine in the fridge), so the recipe doesn't make as big a batch as the others.

Ingredients

2 tbsp olive oil
juice of 1 lemon
2 garlic cloves, crushed
½ in (1 cm) piece fresh ginger, peeled and finely chopped
2 tbsp sweet chili sauce
1 tbsp fish sauce
½ red chili pepper, finely chopped
1 tsp lemongrass purée (optional)

Basil Dressing

Do this one in the blender to get a lovely smooth, thick texture. We would only keep this for a few weeks in the fridge as the basil can get a bit sad and smelly after awhile.

Ingredients

½ cup (120 ml) white wine vinegar
1½ cups (360 ml) extra virgin olive oil
2 tsp brown sugar or honey
handful of basil leaves (about 20)
1 small shallot
2 garlic cloves
salt and black pepper

Blend up all your ingredients in a blender and season to taste.

Acknowledgments

We have had so much help and support from so many people along the way, far too many to list here. But there are some people who have played such a big part in our story that we couldn't not mention them: the Ullapool Harbour Trustees and the harbor master Kevin Peach who have supported us right from our very first meeting; Laura Talbot who silently spent hours helping us with paperwork and still offers any help she can; Richard Ross who helped kit the whole shack out; the community in and around Ullapool who after five years still come and eat our food; our staff who have worked so hard for us over the years, with a special mention to Katie Scobie who has now worked for us for three years and continues to rock up every morning with a smile and huge enthusiasm; our partners and families who support us in any way they can and put up with us smelling of the Shack; and lastly, the fishermen—without them we would be nothing, and they risk their lives on a daily basis to get us what we truly believe is the best produce. When we started the Shack we never in our wildest dreams imagined it being what it is today, so from the bottom of our hearts thank you all so much.

Fenella and Kirsty xxx

Index

Notes

Notes

Notes